T0321669

Querying and
Mining Uncertain
Data Streams

East China Normal University Scientific Reports
Subseries on Data Science and Engineering

ISSN: 2382-5715

Chief Editor
Weian Zheng
Changjiang Chair Professor
School of Finance and Statistics
East China Normal University, China
Email: financialmaths@gmail.com

Associate Chief Editor
Shanping Wang
Senior Editor
Journal of East China Normal University (Natural Sciences), China
Email: spwang@library.ecnu.edu.cn

East China Normal University Scientific Reports | **Vol. 3**
Subseries on Data Science and Engineering

Querying and Mining Uncertain Data Streams

Cheqing Jin
Aoying Zhou

East China Normal University, China

 **World Scientific**

W JERSEY · LONDON · SINGAPORE · BEIJING · SHANGHAI · HONG KONG · TAIPEI · CHENNAI · TOKYO

Published by

World Scientific Publishing Co. Pte. Ltd.

5 Toh Tuck Link, Singapore 596224

USA office: 27 Warren Street, Suite 401-402, Hackensack, NJ 07601

UK office: 57 Shelton Street, Covent Garden, London WC2H 9HE

Library of Congress Cataloging-in-Publication Data

Names: Jin, Cheqing, author. | Zhou, Aoying, 1965–   author.

Title: Querying and mining uncertain data streams / Cheqing Jin (East China Normal University) &
    Aoying Zhou (East China Normal University).

Description: [Hackensack] New Jersey : World Scientific, [2016] | Series: East China Normal
    University scientific reports ; volume 3 | Includes bibliographical references.

Identifiers: LCCN 2015051052| ISBN 9789813108776 (hc : alk. paper) |
    ISBN 9789813108783 (pbk : alk. paper)

Subjects: LCSH: Data mining. | Querying (Computer science) | Uncertainty (Information theory)

Classification: LCC QA76.9.D343 J56 2016 | DDC 006.3/12--dc23

LC record available at http://lccn.loc.gov/2015051052

British Library Cataloguing-in-Publication Data

A catalogue record for this book is available from the British Library.

In-house Editors: Dipasri Sardar/Amanda Yun

Typeset by Stallion Press
Email: enquiries@stallionpress.com

Printed in Singapore

East China Normal University Scientific Reports

Mingkang Ni (Foreign Academician of Russian Academy of Natural Sciences; Professor, Department of Mathematics, East China Normal University)

Zhongming Qian (Zijiang Chair Professor, School of Financial and Statistics, East China Normal University; Lecturer in the Mathematical Institute and Fellow at Exeter College, University of Oxford)

Jiong Shu (Professor, Department of Geography, East China Normal University)

Shengli Tan (Changjiang Chair Professor, Department of Mathematics, East China Normal University)

Peng Wu (Changjiang Scholar Chair Professor, Department of Chemistry, East China Normal University)

Jianpan Wang (Professor, Department of Mathematics, East China Normal University)

Rongming Wang (Professor, School of Financial and Statistics, East China Normal University)

Wei-Ning Xiang (Zijiang Chair Professor, Department of Environmental Science, East China Normal University; Professor, Department of Geography and Earth Science, University of North Carolina at Charlotte)

Danping Yang (Professor, Department of Mathematics, East China Normal University)

Kai Yang (Professor, Department of Environmental Science, East China Normal University)

Shuyi Zhang (Zijiang Chair Professor, School of Life Sciences, East China Normal University)

Weiping Zhang (Changjiang Chair Professor, Department of Physics, East China Normal University)

Xiangming Zheng (Professor, Department of Geography, East China Normal University)

Aoying Zhou (Changjiang Chair Professor, Software Engineering Institute, East China Normal University)

Subseries on Data Science and Engineering

Chief Editor

Aoying Zhou
Changjiang Chair Professor
Software Engineering Institute
East China Normal University, China
Email: ayzhou@sei.ecnu.edu.cn

Associate Editors

Rakesh Agrawal (Technical Fellow, Microsoft Research in Silicon Valley)
Michael Franklin (University of California at Berkeley)
H. V, Jagadish (University of Michigan in Ann Arbor)
Christian S. Jensen (University of Aalborg)
Masaru Kitsuregawa (University of Tokyo, National Institute of Informatics (NII))
Volker Markl (Technische Universität Berlin (TU Berlin))
Gerhard Weikum (Max Planck Institute for Informatics)
Ruqian Lu (Academy of Mathematics and Systems Science, Chinese Academy of Sciences)

Preface

With the rapid development of economy, big data becomes an important phenomenon in many applications recently. In general, big data is treated as having three characteristics, including *volume*, *velocity*, and *variety*. *Volume* means the size of data is huge, *velocity* means data arrives rapidly, and *variety* means data has multiple styles of representation. Data stream is a data sequence that arrives rapidly with unbounded volume in assumption. How to query and mining data stream efficiently has been studied for a long time.

Data uncertainty is another important character of big data, due to many causes, such as low-end physical equipments, manual intervention, data missing, and data integration. There are two kinds of uncertainties, including existential uncertainty and attribute-level uncertainty. Hence, querying and mining uncertain data streams become critical due to the imprecise nature of the data generated from a variety of streaming applications. However, it is non-trivial to devise efficient solutions to deal with such issues, since the challenge not only comes from the strict space and time requirements of processing arriving (and expiring) tuples in high-speed streams, but also comes from the exponential blowup in the number of possible worlds induced by the uncertain data model. In this book, the following issues are addressed.

- *Top-k queries over the sliding-window model.* We design a unified framework to process sliding-window top-k queries on uncertain streams, into which some existing top-k definitions in the literature can be plugged, resulting in several succinct synopses that use space much smaller than the window size, while they are also highly efficient in terms of processing time.

- *ER-Topk query over the landmark model.* As a special uncertain top-k query, ER-Top$k$ uses the expected rank to rank all tuples in a data stream. We construct three data structures to process ER-Top$k$ continuously, including a graph (DomGraph), a binary tree (probTree) and a buffer (ES buffer). The former one is used to store all potential tuples, and the latter two are used to compute the exact and approximate values of expected rank.

- *Rarity estimation.* Rarity describes the proportion of items with same frequency upon uncertain data. We propose two methods (including an exact one and an approximate one) to compute the rarity of a given frequency, and one method to find the frequency of the maximal rarity.

- *Set similarity computation.* Set similarity describes the similarity between two probabilistic sets, where each probabilistic set may have thousands of elements. We define two types of similarities, complementing each other in capturing the similarity distributions in the cross product of possible worlds. Our first solution is capable of computing the set similarity exactly, and our second solution is a sampling-based approximate query processing method with strong probabilistic guarantees to accommodate extremely large probabilistic sets.

- *Clustering.* Clustering aims at dividing a large set into some clusters with inner-cluster distance minimized and inter-cluster distance maximized. We propose a data structure (Uncertain Feature, UF) to summarize data streams with both kinds of uncertainties. We try to enhance the previous streaming approaches to handle the sliding-window model by using UF instead of old synopses, inclusive of CluStream and UMicro. Moreover, we propose a novel algorithm (cluUS) that outperforms the above methods.

Shanghai, China   *Cheqing Jin*
September, 2014   *Aoying Zhou*

Acknowledgments

This research was supported by 973 plan (No. 2012CB316203) and the National Science Foundation of China (Nos. 60803020, 60933001, 61070052 and 61370101).

We thank all friends, Feng Cao, Lei Chen, Ming Gao, Xuemin Lin, Wei Wang, Ke Yi, Jeffrey Xu Yu, Jingwei Zhang, and Minqi Zhou, without whom the technical contributions of this book cannot be worked out.

We thank Kun Yue, who gave valuable suggestions on how to organize a book.

We would like to express our sincere thanks and appreciation to the people at Springer US, for their generous help throughout the publication preparation process.

Contents

About the Authors

 **Cheqing Jin** is Professor of Software Engineering at East China Normal University (ECNU). He received his master and bachelor degrees from Zhejiang University, China, in 1999 and 2002 respectively, and his PhD degree from Fudan University, China, in 2005 — all in Computer Science. He worked as an Assistant Professor in East China University of Science and Technology from 2005 to 2008, after which he joined ECNU in October 2008. In 2003 and 2007, he visited the Hong Kong University and the Chinese University of Hong Kong, respectively. His work has been published in various leading conference and journals, such as the International Conference on Very Large Data Bases (VLDB), the International Conference on Data Engineering (ICDE), and The VLDB Journal. Prof Jin was awarded the Young Teacher Award by the Fok Ying Tong Education Foundation in 2015. His main research interests include streaming data management, location-based services, uncertain data management, data quality, and database benchmarking.

 **Aoying Zhou** is Professor of Software Engineering at East China Normal University (ECNU), where he heads the Institute for Data Science and Engineering. He received his master and bachelor degrees in Computer Science from Sichuan University, China, in 1988 and 1985 respectively, and his PhD degree from Fudan University, China, in 1993. Before joining ECNU in 2008, Aoying worked for Fudan University in the Computer Science Department for 15 years. He is the winner of the National Science Fund for Distinguished Young Scholars supported by the National Natural Science Foundation of China (NSFC), as well as the professorship appointment under the Changjiang Scholars Program of the Ministry of Education, China. He is now acting as a vice-director of ACM SIGMOD (Association for Computing Machinery's Special Interest Group on Management of Data) China, and the Database Technology Committee of the China Computer Federation. Prof Zhou is a serving member of the editorial boards of journals such as The VLDB Journal and World Wide Web Journal, amongst others. His research interests include web data management, data management for data-intensive computing, memory cluster computing, benchmarking for big data, and performance.

Chapter 1

Introduction

1.1 Background

During the past four decades, huge efforts have been dedicated to manage data that is deterministic, and the successful deployment of commercial DBMSs deeply influences human life. Most recently, it becomes critical to process uncertain (probabilistic) data, since data uncertainty widely exists in many applications, such as economy, military, logistic, finance, and telecommunication, etc. The causes for uncertain data include, but are not limited to the following: low-end physical equipments, manual intervention, data missing, and data integration [82].

- *Low-end physical equipments.* Data may be imprecise due to low-end physical equipments, such as sensor networks [29]. Data accuracy is also affected by bandwidth, transmission delay and energy during wireless network transmission process. It is reported that more than 30% of tag readings in the RFID applications are dropped [46].
- *Manual intervention.* Manual intervention helps to achieve special targets, such as privacy preserving. For example, modern GPS-enabled electronic devices can track the trajectories of moving objects, such as intelligent mobile phones. A common way to protect location privacy (called k-anonymity) uses an area to describe the actual location of a user, so that he (she) cannot be distinguished from the other $k - 1$ users.

1

- *Data missing.* Data missing occurs in many cases, including equipment failure, invalid access, data inconsistent, and historical usage. Although some existing data cleaning mechanisms can eliminate uncertainty by assuming the underlying data follows a distribution or simply ignoring incomplete records, they cannot describe the nature of data uncertainty well.
- *Data integration.* Data integration also brings in uncertainty, since the data from different sources may be inconsistent. By integrating multiple sources of uncertain data, it is helpful to resolve portions of the uncertainty to achieve more accurate results [7].

A significant trend in the modern applications is that the uncertain data tends to be gathered in a streaming fashion. For example, each sensor node in a senor network gathers and transfers data to a main site continuously; RFID tags are read continuously. Table 1.1 illustrates a small example of modern traffic monitoring applications, where radars are used to detect the speed of vehicles. There are four tuples, each described as a discrete probability distribution function rather than a single value, since some errors may be caused for complicated reasons, such as nearby high voltage lines, close cars' interference, human operator mistakes, etc. For instance, the 1st record observes a Buick car (No. Z-333) running through the monitoring area at 10:33 AM with the speed estimated as 50 (miles per hour) with probability 0.6, and 70 with probability 0.4 respectively. In addition, a range is used to test the validation of a speed reading (e.g., [0, 120]). Once the reading exceeds the range, this information is removed from the tuple description, which makes the total confidence smaller than 1. For example, the 3rd record

Table 1.1   A Radar Reading Data Stream

ID	Reading Info	(speed, probability)
1	10:33 AM, Buick, Z-333	(50, 0.6), (70, 0.4)
2	10:35 AM, BMW, X-215	(60, 1.0)
3	10:37 AM, Benz, X-511	(80, 0.4)
4	10:38 AM, Mazda, Y-123	(20, 0.4), (30, 0.5)

estimates the speed of 80 with probability 0.4, and of invalidation with probability 0.6 $(= 1 - 0.4)$.

There are two kinds of uncertainties: *attribute-level* uncertainty and *existential* uncertainty. The latter is also called as *tuple-level* uncertainty in some literatures [2]. The *attribute-level* uncertainty, commonly described as discrete probability distribution function or probability density function, illustrates the imprecision of a tuple's attributes, e.g., the first tuple. The *existential* uncertainty describes the confidence of a tuple, e.g., the third tuple. A tuple may have two kinds of uncertainties at the same time, such as the last tuple.

Uncertain data streams have attracted a lot of attention [5, 20, 44, 45, 78]. Since large amounts of such streaming data arrive rapidly, the goal is to design both space- and time-efficient query processing techniques, which only require to visit each tuple once. On the other hand, streaming data is also highly time-sensitive: people are generally more interested in the recent tuples than those in the far past, which further adds the challenges of uncertain stream processing.

1.2 Data Model

The model for uncertain data streams is actually the integration of data uncertainty and streaming property. Most uncertain data models adopt the possible world semantics [1, 36], in which the possible world space contains a huge number of possible world instances (also shorten as possible world), each consisting of a set of certain values from uncertain tuples. A possible world instance is affiliated with a probability value, computed by the product of all tuples within the instance and the product of the non-existing confidence of all tuples outside.

Table 1.2 illustrates the possible world space of total 12 instances for the data stream in Table 1.1. Each column is a possible world instance with the probability listed below. For example, tuples t_1, t_2 and t_3 occur in pw_{10} at the same time, while t_4 does not occur, so the probability of pw_{10} is computed as 0.016 $(= 0.4 \times 1.0 \times 0.4 \times (1 - 0.4 - 0.5))$.

Table 1.2 The Possible World Space for Table 1.1

Possible world	pw_1	pw_2	pw_3	pw_4	pw_5	pw_6	pw_7	pw_8	pw_9	pw_{10}	pw_{11}	pw_{12}
t_1	50	70	50	70	50	70	50	70	50	70	50	70
t_2	60	60	60	60	60	60	60	60	60	60	60	60
t_3	80	80	—	—	80	80	—	—	80	80	—	—
t_4	20	20	20	20	30	30	30	30	—	—	—	—
Probability	0.096	0.064	0.144	0.096	0.120	0.080	0.150	0.120	0.024	0.016	0.036	0.024

In general, an uncertain stream S is defined as $S = \{t_1, t_2, \ldots\}$, where an uncertain tuple t_i appears at timestamp i. Each tuple is described as a discrete probability distribution function, $t_i = \langle (v_{i,1}, p_{i,1}), \ldots, (v_{i,m_i}, p_{i,m_i}) \rangle$, meaning that t_i can be one of m_i different certain values, denoted as $v_{i,1}, \ldots, v_{i,m_i}$, with confidence of $p_{i,1}, \ldots, p_{i,m_i}$. The sum of the probabilities of all choices is no greater than 1, i.e., $\forall i, \sum_{j=1}^{m_i} p_{i,j} \leq 1$. Especially, if only existential uncertainty exists, $\forall i \geq 1$, $m_i = 1$ [20].

The streaming models can be categorized into the *landmark*, *time-decay*, and *sliding-window* models according to time aspect. The *landmark* model considers all tuples from a fixed time point to now. The *time-decay* model assigns a weight to each tuple, and the weight will decrease over time. This model usually works together with statistical aggregates, such as averages, histograms, and heavy hitters [21, 24]. The *sliding-window* model only considers all tuples within a pre-defined window W. In other words, the rest ones outside the window are filtered. For example, assuming $W = 5$, the window is $[6, 10]$ at time 10.

One major challenge of uncertain data management is that the possible world space will grow up exponentially to the size of the uncertain database. Suppose there are N independent tuples in an uncertain database, the number of the possible world instances is $O(2^N)$. Hence, it is infeasible to access all possible world instances one by one even when N is not tiny. Therefore, it is necessary to make a trade-off between the accuracy and overhead, so as to obtain high-quality approximate results with small computational overhead. Moreover, the possible world space will change a lot when a new tuple

Table 1.3 The Possible World Space for Table 1.1 over the Sliding-window Model ($W = 3$)

(a) At time 3

Possible world	pw_1	pw_2	pw_3	pw_4
t_1	50	70	50	70
t_2	60	60	60	60
t_3	80	80	—	—
Probability	0.24	0.16	0.36	0.24

(b) At time 4

Possible world	pw_1	pw_2	pw_3	pw_4	pw_5	pw_6
t_2	60	60	60	60	60	60
t_3	80	80	80	—	—	—
t_4	20	30	—	20	30	—
Probability	0.16	0.20	0.04	0.24	0.30	0.06

arrives, no matter upon the landmark model or the sliding-window model. For example, assuming $W = 3$, Tables 1.3(a) and 1.3(b) show the possible world space for the data in Table 1.1 at times 3 and 4 respectively. We observe that all possible world instances change.

Furthermore, we also study a more comprehensive model in Chapter 5 where each tuple in the data stream is no longer a single value, but a set of probabilistic tuples. An example data stream may be: $\{\{1 : 0.7, 2, 1.0\}, \{2 : 0.5, 3 : 0.7, 4 : 0.4\}, \ldots\}$. In this stream, the first set, $\{1 : 0.7, 2, 1.0\}$, contains two tuples, 1 and 2, each with probability 0.7 and 1.0. The second set in the data stream contains three tuples, and so on. Similarly, we can construct a joint-possible world space based on any of two probabilistic sets.

For example, consider two probabilistic sets A and B in Table 1.4. They have eight (joint) possible worlds, which are listed together with their similarities and existential probabilities in Table 1.4(b). For example, the 2nd possible world is made up of $\{2^A\}$ and $\{1^B, 2^B\}$. The former's existential probability is $(1 - 0.7) \cdot 1 = 0.3$, and the latter's existential probability is $1 \cdot 0.5 \cdot (1 - 0.8) = 0.1$. Therefore, the existential probability of the joint possible world is $0.3 \cdot 0.1 = 0.03$.

Table 1.4 The Joint Possible Worlds upon Two Probabilistic Sets

(a) Two probabilistic sets

A	B
$\{1:0.7,\ 2:1.0\}$	$\{1:1.0,\ 2:0.5,\ 3:0.8\}$

(b) All the joint possible worlds with non-zero probabilities (e^X is the element e of p-set X)

pw_a	pw_b	$\Pr(pw_a, pw_b)$
$\{2^A\}$	$\{1^B\}$	0.03
$\{2^A\}$	$\{1^B, 2^B\}$	0.03
$\{2^A\}$	$\{1^B, 3^B\}$	0.12
$\{2^A\}$	$\{1^B, 2^B, 3^B\}$	0.12
$\{2^A, 1^A\}$	$\{1^B\}$	0.07
$\{2^A, 1^A\}$	$\{1^B, 2^B\}$	0.07
$\{2^A, 1^A\}$	$\{1^B, 3^B\}$	0.28
$\{2^A, 1^A\}$	$\{1^B, 2^B, 3^B\}$	0.28

1.3 Important Issues

Top-k query. Top-k query is fundamental in database management field. Given a ranking function, the goal of uncertain top-k query is to find the top-k ranked tuples in an uncertain dataset. However, most of the existing approaches are designed for static data, not for streaming data, and it is infeasible to directly apply such solutions to the streaming scenario, since they require to store all tuples in memory, which consumes too much memory space.

We first design a unified framework to process continuous top-k queries over the sliding-window model, into which several uncertain top-k definitions can be plugged. Our framework is composed of several space- and time-efficient synopses with provable bounds. To cope with tuples expiring, we need a carefully designed synopsis storing the minimal amount of information yet still sufficient for answering the query continuously at all times, which should also be maintained efficiently [49, 50].

We next study ER-Top$k$ over the landmark model. ER-Top$k$ query uses the expected rank to rank each tuple in the dataset.

However, a tuple's expected rank may change when new tuples come, which makes it more challenging in the streaming scenario. We construct three novel structures, including *domGraph*, *probTree* and *ES* buffer. The first one stores all candidate tuples with highest ranks, while the rest help to compute the rank of each tuple [48,52].

Rarity estimation. Rarity is important in uncertain data environments. For example, some factories may deploy a number of sensors to monitor environment. In general, these sensors report *normal* state. But when the environment changes, some sensors will report different kinds of abnormal states, rather than *normal*. *Rarity* can be used to detect this event.

We made the first attempt to study rarity upon uncertain data. First, we extend the semantics of rarity to uncertain data by adopting the possible world semantics. Our first solution computes the rarity value exactly by using dynamic programming with space consumption $O(m^2)$ and time complexity $O(m^3)$, where m is the number of distinct elements in the dataset. Our second solution estimates the rarity by using Monte Carlo technique, which is both space- and time-efficient. We study how to find the frequency with maximal rarity. After using some heuristic rules, it is merely necessary to compute a part of rarity values, not all rarity values [53].

Set similarity. Similarity query processing is a fundamental and active research area in databases. There are methods to abstract objects into either a multidimensional vector or a set of feature values. Similarity between objects then can be evaluated as similarity or distance between their computerized representations, which is amenable to many optimization techniques, such as indexing and top-k query optimization. While there exists abundant research work in similarity query processing for certain sets, there are only few studies on probabilistic sets. Probabilistic sets arise naturally out of applications where data may contain noise, data values are inherently imprecise, or data values are summarized, so that the existence of an element in a set is characterized by its existential probability.

We systematically study the problem of modeling uncertainty in sets with the aim to support large probabilistic sets. We model a probabilistic set, or a *p*-set, as a set of elements, each with its existential probability. We propose an intuitive yet expressive model for probabilistic sets appearing in many real applications. Our proposed model complements the existing ones by supporting applications that need to handle large p-sets due to the computational efficiency. We define two types of similarity measures to capture different characteristics of the similarity distributions between two p-sets under the possible world semantics. We first propose a method to compute similarity exactly. Besides, we also propose sampling-based algorithms to approximate the similarity between two p-sets with probabilistic guarantees [33].

Clustering. Clustering has been studied for a long time, aiming at dividing a dataset into a number of clusters with inner-cluster distance minimized and inter-cluster distance maximized. However, most previous work on clustering uncertain data needs to scan the whole dataset more than once, so that these methods cannot be applied to streaming scenarios directly. Few existing clustering methods can handle the sliding-window model [5].

We propose a new space-efficient synopsis data structure to summarize uncertain data with both kinds of uncertainties, with which important statistics can be computed efficiently, such as central point, root mean square distance from centroid, root mean square distance between all pairs of points, inter-cluster distance, intra-cluster distance, etc. Then, we upgrade two existing methods to handle the sliding-window model. Finally, we propose a more efficient algorithm by maintaining some micro-clusters in the buffer [51].

1.4 Related Work

Recently, querying and processing uncertain data streams have been more and more important in various applications, such as Web, sensor networks, etc. [2, 26]. Typical work includes aggregation [20, 44, 53], data mining [5, 78], skyline [80], ranking query [48, 49] and so on. Good surveys on recent uncertain data algorithms are [2, 6]. Jayram *et al.* study some basic aggregation operators, such as sum, count, avg, max, and min [44]. Cormode and Garofalakis study some complicated aggregation operators by building synopsis data structures, such as F_0, F_2, and quantile [20]. [53] studies how to compute rarity on uncertain data. In [5], Aggarwal and Yu propose a framework to cluster uncertain data streams. Zhang *et al.* propose exact and approximate solutions to mine frequent items over uncertain streams [78]. In [80], Zhang *et al.* study how to process skyline query in the sliding-window model. The PODS system is developed to support relational processing of uncertain data streams modeled using continuous random variables [73]. In [72], Tran *et al.* study how to evaluate queries involving conditioning operations and aggregates [72]. Moreover, there are a lot of efforts in extending the query processing techniques from static uncertain data to uncertain data streams [5, 20, 21, 24, 44, 45, 78]. Related work on top-k query, rarity, set similarity, and clustering are reviewed below.

Top-k query. Top-k queries on a traditional certain dataset are well studied in the literature [32,65]. The threshold algorithm (TA) [65] is one of the best known algorithms. It assumes each tuple has several attributes, and the ranking function is monotonous on them. TA first sorts the tuples by each attribute and then scans the sorted lists in parallel. When a new tuple appears, TA looks it up in all lists to update its rank. In addition, TA maintains a "stopping value", which acts as a threshold to prune the tuples in the rest of the lists if they cannot have better scores than the threshold.

There are many recent development and extensions to top-k queries under different scenarios. Babcock and Olston [12] propose an algorithm to monitor the top-k most frequent items in a distributed environment. Das *et al.* [27] use views to answer top-k queries efficiently. Xin *et al.* [74] remove redundancy in top-k patterns. Xin *et al.* [75] also apply multidimensional analysis in top-k queries. Hua *et al.* [40] define the rank of a tuple by the typicality and answer the top-k typicality queries. A very relevant work to ours is the paper by Mouratidis *et al.* [63], which presents a method to continuously monitor top-k queries over sliding windows. However, same as all of the other works listed above, it only considers certain databases.

There are different definitions for uncertain top-k queries based on a ranking function. Soliman *et al.* [71] first define two types of such top-k queries, named U-Top$k$ and U-kRanks, and proposed algorithms for each of them. Their algorithms were subsequently improved by Yi *et al.* [77]. Hua *et al.* [41, 42] propose another top-k definition, namely PT-k, and proposed efficient solutions. The Pk-Top$k$ query that we mainly focus on in this paper is actually a slight variant of PT-k. The ER-Top$k$ query proposed by Cormode *et al.* ranks each tuple by the expected rank [22]. Other representative definitions include ES-top$k$ [22], UTop-Set$k$ [70], c-Typical-Top$k$ [34], unified top$k$ [59]. However, most existing work cannot deal with the streaming scenario, which turns to be our focus.

Rarity. The α-rarity of a dataset returns the proportion of tuples occurring α times in a dataset. Datar and Muthukrishnan estimate the rarity over sliding window by using min-wise hashing [28]. Their work mainly aims at devising an approximate one-pass solution upon deterministic data. To the best of our knowledge, there is no prior work on computing rarity upon uncertain data till now. To some extent, the concept of the rarity relates to the general issue of non-conforming patterns in data, such as anomaly, outlier, exception and so on [17]. Different from the rarity, these concepts aim at discovering some concrete instances (or objects).

Set similarity. A similarity search, which returns objects similar or close to a query object, is a well-researched topic in the literature. Compared with the vast amount of similarity search research on certain data, there is relatively small amount of work on uncertain data. [14,78] propose the frequent item mining on uncertain data. Pei *et al.* propose skyline query on uncertain data [68]. Xu *et al.* study similarity search based on the Earth Mover's Distance (EMD) [76]. It is popular to use probabilistic models to capture many alternatives during the Optical Character Recognition (OCR) process. Kumar and Ré [58] proposes an approximation scheme to trade recall for query performance. There have been a few studies on similarity joins over uncertain data [47, 55, 60, 62]. Kriegel *et al.* study probabilistic spatial similarity join on uncertain data, where probabilistic distance functions are used to measure the similarity between uncertain objects [55]. Josa and Singh [62] studies two kinds of Probabilistic Spatial Join (PSJ) over uncertain data: the threshold PSJ and top-k PSJ.

There also exists some work on similarity joins upon probabilistic sets [47,60,81]. Zhang *et al.* [81] considers efficient query processing methods for set containment queries for probabilistic sets. One of the similarity measures considered (expected Jaccard containment) and its dynamic programming-based computation algorithm are similar to our expected Jaccard similarity and its computation algorithm [33]. Jestes *et al.* [47] investigates the problem of probabilistic similarity joins over strings regarding the expected edit distance measure (EED), and a set of novel techniques have been developed. Lian and Chen [60] studies the similarity between two probabilistic sets. After defining two probabilistic models, set-level model and element-level model, some pruning rules are proposed to hasten query processing. Our work is significantly different from such work [33]. Zhang *et al.* [81] does not consider pruning method for individual sets or batch pruning, nor do they consider approximate query processing methods, as the probabilistic sets considered contain small number of elements (up to 25). There are several major technical differences between [47] and ours. For example, although character-level uncertain strings are decomposed into probabilistic sets of q-grams, there are non-neglectible correlations among these elements. In addition, the major technical challenge in [47] is to establish lower and upper bounds for EED based on some functions involving aggregated probabilities of constituent q-grams. The pruning rules proposed in [33] are significantly more powerful than those proposed in [60].

Clustering. Clustering has been intensively studied with many proposed solutions, such as DBSCAN [31], CURE [38] and BIRCH [79]. After realizing the importance of data streams, some researchers also extend their work to cluster a data stream with economical space consumption, such as STREAM [67], SWKM [11], CluStream [4], etc. How to cluster uncertain data has also been studied intensively [18, 23, 56, 57, 66]. In [56, 57], density-based algorithms, FDBSCAN and FOPTICS, are proposed. The Uk-means algorithm [18] is used to cluster uncertain data by extending traditional k-means algorithm. The fuzzy c-means algorithm studies another problem that the memberships of a tuple can belong to more than one cluster [30]. The work in [66] improves the performance of Uk-means by developing a pruning technique to speed up the computation of the expected distance between a pair of tuples [66]. The work in [54] uses Voronoi diagrams to improve the performance of Uk-means. Cormode and McGregor propose approximate algorithms to cluster uncertain data with guaranteed errors [23].

However, methods above need to visit data more than once, thus none can handle uncertain streams. The clustering algorithm by Aggarwal and Yu [5] is an extension of their micro-clustering technique [4], where the mean and variance of a micro-cluster are maintained carefully. However, their work only considers attribute-level uncertainty, not existential uncertainty. Aggarwal [3] proposes a method on high dimensional projected clustering of uncertain data streams.

1.5 Organization

The rest of this book is organized below. In Chapters 2 and 3, we study top-k query over the sliding-window model and the landmark model respectively. In Chapter 4, we show how to estimate rarity over a data stream. In Chapter 5, we propose some methods to compute set similarity. Subsequently, in Chapter 6, we study clustering over the sliding-window model. Finally, we conclude the book briefly in the last chapter.

Chapter 2

Top-k Queries Over
the Sliding-window Model

2.1 Problem Definition

Let S be an uncertain stream containing a sequence of tuples, $t_1, t_2, \ldots, t_N$, where the subscripts denote the timestamps of the tuples. Let f be a ranking function. We use $t_i \prec_f t_j$ if $f(t_i) > f(t_j)$, and we say t_i's rank is higher than t_j's. In a similar fashion, $t_i \succ_f t_j$ means t_i's rank is lower than t_j's. Without loss of generality, we assume that the ranks of all tuples are unique. The membership probability of tuple t is denoted as $p(t)$.

A sliding window starting at position i and ending at j is denoted as $S[i, j]$, i.e., $S[i, j] = (t_i, t_{i+1}, \ldots, t_j)$, for $i \leq j$. This window will slide to $S[i+1, j+1]$ at the next time stamp. The size of the sliding window is $W = j - i + 1$. For the sliding window $S[i, j]$, $PW(S[i, j])$ denotes its possible world space $PW(S[i, j]) = \{pw_1, pw_2, \ldots\}$, where each entry is a possible world that is a subset of tuples in $S[i, j]$. The probability of such a possible world pw is given as $\mathbf{Pr}[pw] = \prod_{t \in pw} p(t) \times \prod_{t \notin pw} (1 - p(t))$.

Definition 2.1. *Probabilistic k top-k query (Pk-topk)*: Let D denote an uncertain database, $PW(D)$ the possible world space for D. Let $PW(t) \subseteq PW(D)$ denote the set of possible worlds containing t as one of its top-k ranked tuples. A Pk-top$k$ query returns a set of k tuples $T = \{t^1, \ldots, t^k\}$, satisfying $\sum_{pw \in PW(t^i)} \mathbf{Pr}[pw] \geq \sum_{pw \in PW(t^j)} \mathbf{Pr}[pw]$, for any $t^i \in T$ and $t^j \notin T$.

13

The goal here is to answer the top-k query for every sliding window $S[i - W + 1, i]$ as i goes from W to N. For now we will use tuple-based windows, where at time i, t_i arrives while t_{i-W} expires. But all our algorithms can be easily extended to time-based windows. We will mostly focus on the Pk-top$k$ query, but will also discuss extensions to the other queries in Section 2.4. As with all streaming algorithms [9], memory consumption is the most important measure; but at the same time, we would like the processing time per tuple to be as low as possible.

2.2 Compact Set

This section first defines the *compact set*, a basic concept in all our synopses. It turns out if there are only insertions, one single compact set is sufficient for maintaining the top-k answers. However, we need multiple compact sets combined together to cope with expiring tuples.

Suppose the tuples in an uncertain dataset D are $t^1 \prec_f \cdots \prec_f t^n$. Denote by D_i the subset of D containing the first i tuples in D, $D_i = \{t^1, \ldots, t^i\}$. For $0 \le j \le i \le n$, let $r_{i,j}$ be the probability that a randomly generated world from D_i has exactly j tuples. It is clear that the probability that t^i ranks the jth in a randomly generated world from D is $p(t^i) \cdot r_{i-1,j-1}$.

Definition 2.2. The *compact set* $C(D)$ for the Pk-top$k$ query on an uncertain dataset D is the smallest subset of D that satisfies the following conditions. (1) $\forall t' \in C(D)$ and $t'' \in D - C(D)$, $t' \prec_f t''$. (2) Let $d = |C(D)|$, t^d the tuple with the lowest rank in $C(D)$. There are k tuples in $C(D)$, and each such tuple t^α has

$$p(t^\alpha) \sum_{1 \le l \le k} r_{\alpha-1,l-1} \ge \sum_{1 \le l \le k} r_{d,l-1}. \tag{2.1}$$

Observe that the LHS (left-hand side) of Equation (2.1) is the probability that tuple t^α is a top-k element, and the RHS (right-hand side) of (2.1) is the maximal probability of any tuple outside $C(D)$ being a top-k element. Therefore, if we have a compact set

$C(D)$, then any other element not in $C(D)$ has no chance of being in the top-k. However, note that some D may not have a compact set, that is, even if we put all tuples into $C(D)$, condition (2) still cannot be satisfied. When this happens, it means that D is not "safe" in the sense that, if a new tuple (even with the lowest rank) is added to D, it is still possible for it to become a top-k element. On the other hand, when there exists a $C(D)$ such that condition (2) holds, we say that D *admits* a compact set, and in this case, we can safely discard any new tuple whose rank is lower than those in the compact set.

It is not difficult to obtain the following recursion [41, 77]:

$$r_{i,j} = \begin{cases} p(t^i)r_{i-1,j-1} + (1 - p(t^i))r_{i-1,j}, & i \geq j \geq 0; \\ 1, & i = j = 0; \\ 0, & \text{else.} \end{cases} \quad (2.2)$$

Thus we can use dynamic programming to compute all the entries in the array r, as well as $C(D)$, in time $O(kd)$. The importance of a compact set $C(D)$ is that we do not need to look at tuples not in $C(D)$ in order to answer a Pk-top$k$ query. Except for some pathological cases, the compact set almost always exists and is much smaller than the whole dataset. So answering a top-k query is usually quite efficient, and we do not need to look at the entire dataset at all, assuming the tuples are already sorted in rank order.

Example 2.1. Consider a Pk-top$k$ query over the dataset in Table 2.1(a), $k = 2$. After sorting, $t^1 = 8$, $t^2 = 6$, $t^3 = 5$, and $t^4 = 2$. Applying Equation (2.2), we calculate the array r using dynamic programming, as listed in Table 2.1(b). In fact, there is no need to generate the right three columns because $j \geq k$. Now, we find that when $d < 3$, there does not exist any tuple t^α ($\alpha \leq d$) satisfying Equation (2.1). When $d = 3$, the RHS of Equation (2.1) is: $0.06 + 0.34 = 0.4$, and the LHS of Equation (2.1) for all of three tuples (t^1, t^2, and t^3) are 0.4, 0.5, and 0.64, respectively, which means that all of them are valid t^α's. So, the compact set for this dataset is $\{t^3, t^2, t^1\}$.

Table 2.1   An Example of Uncertain Top-k Query

(a) A data stream

ID	Reading Info	Speed ($\times 10$)	prob.
1	10:33 AM, Honda, X-123	5	0.8
2	10:35 AM, Toyota, Y-245	6	0.5
3	10:37 AM, Mazda, Z-341	8	0.4
4	10:38 AM, Benz, W-541	2	0.4

(b) The array $r_{i,j}$ for Table 2.1(a)

$r_{i,j}$	$j = 0$	$j = 1$	$j = 2$	$j = 3$	$j = 4$
$i = 0$	1	0	0	0	0
$i = 1$	0.6	0.4	0	0	0
$i = 2$	0.3	0.5	0.2	0	0
$i = 3$	0.06	0.34	0.44	0.16	0
$i = 4$	0.036	0.228	0.4	0.272	0.064

However, [41, 42, 77] only consider the static case. It is not clear at all whether this compact set can be self-maintained as tuples are inserted into D. It turns out that to answer this question, a much more careful analysis is required.

Self-maintenance of the compact set. We first need to study some important characteristics of the array r. We also study the change ratio $q_{i,j}$ of adjacent entries for any tuple t_i, namely $q_{i,j} = \frac{r_{i,j+1}}{r_{i,j}}$, where $i \geq j \geq 0$. Specifically, we have the following properties.

Property 2.1. The value of $q_{i,j}$ is monotonically decreasing for any tuple t_i, i.e., $r_{i,j}^2 \geq r_{i,j-1} \cdot r_{i,j+1}$, for $j \geq 1$.

Property 2.2. For any two tuples t_i, t_j satisfying $t_i \prec_f t_j$, we have $q_{i,l} \leq q_{j,l}$, where $l \geq 0$, i.e., $r_{i,l+1} r_{j,l} \leq r_{i,l} r_{j,l+1}$.

Property 2.3. For any tuple t_i, the series $r_{i,j}$ is unimodal, i.e., there exists some m such that $r_{i,j}$ is monotonically increasing when $j < m$ while monotonically decreasing when $j > m$.

Property 2.4. For any tuples t_i, t_j, $t_i \prec_f t_j$. The peak point of the corresponding series (in Property 2.3) for t_i is no later than t_j.

Table 2.2 The Array $q_{i,j}$ for Table 2.1(b)

$q_{i,j}$	$j = 0$	$j = 1$	$j = 2$	$j = 3$	$j = 4$
$i = 0$	0	—	—	—	—
$i = 1$	0.67	0	—	—	—
$i = 2$	1.67	0.4	0	—	—
$i = 3$	5.67	1.29	0.36	0	—
$i = 4$	6.3	1.75	0.68	0.24	0

Example 2.2. Table 2.2 shows the values of $q_{i,j}$ based on Table 2.1(a). Property 2.1 says that the value of $q_{i,j}$ is monotonically decreasing along each row, while Property 2.2 says that the value of $q_{i,j}$ is monotonically increasing along each column. Because $q_{1,0}$, $q_{2,1}$, $q_{3,2}$ and $q_{4,2}$ are the first entries smaller than 1 at each row, the corresponding positions at $r_{i,j}$ (Table 2.1(a)) are peak points at each row (Property 2.3). In addition, the column-values of peak points are monotonically increasing, i.e., 0, 1, 2, 2 in Table 2.1(a) (Property 2.4).

Theorem 2.1. *Let $C(D)$ be the compact set of D, let t^d be the lowest-rank tuple in $C(D)$, and let t_{new} be a new tuple to be inserted into D. Then $C(D \cup \{t_{new}\}) = C(D)$ if $t^d \prec_f t_{new}$, and $C(D \cup \{t_{new}\}) \subseteq C(D) \cup \{t_{new}\}$ if $t_{new} \prec_f t^d$.*

Proof. Let r' be the array for $C(D) \cup \{t_{new}\}$. Let us consider the following cases in turn.

Case 1: $t_{new} \succ_f t^d$. Then $r_{i,j} = r'_{i,j}$ for all $1 \leq i \leq d$, so $r_{\alpha-1,l-1}$ and $r_{d,l-1}$ remain unchanged for $1 \leq l \leq k$. Thus, $C(D \cup \{t_{new}\}) = C(D)$.

Case 2: For all the t^α that meets (2.1), $t^d \succ_f t_{new} \succ_f t^\alpha$. We will show that (2.1) still holds on r'. For $1 \leq l \leq k$, we have

$$r'_{d,l-1} = p(t_{new})r_{d,l-2} + (1 - p(t_{new}))r_{d,l-1}.$$

Summing over all l,

$$\sum_{l=1}^{k} r'_{d,l-1} = \sum_{l=1}^{k} r_{d,l-1} - p(t_{new})r_{d,k-1}, \qquad (2.3)$$

namely, the RHS of (2.1) is reduced while its LHS stays the same. So (2.1) still holds on r', hence $C(D \cup \{t_{new}\}) \subseteq C(D) \cup \{t_{new}\}$.

Case 3: There exists one or more t^α that meet (2.1) such that $t^\alpha \succ_f t_{new}$. Now both the LHS and RHS of (2.1) change, so we need to be more careful.

First, for any such t^α, we have

$$r'_{\alpha-1,l-1} = p(t_{new})r_{\alpha-1,l-2} + (1 - p(t_{new}))r_{\alpha-1,l-1}.$$

Summing over all l,

$$\sum_{l=1}^{k} r'_{\alpha-1,l-1} = \sum_{l=1}^{k} r_{\alpha-1,l-1} - p(t_{new})r_{\alpha-1,k-1}.$$

So, the LHS of (2.1) decreases by a fraction of

$$1 - \frac{p(t^\alpha)\sum_{l=1}^{k} r'_{\alpha-1,l-1}}{p(t^\alpha)\sum_{l=1}^{k} r_{\alpha-1,l-1}} = p(t_{new})\frac{r_{\alpha-1,k-1}}{\sum_{l=1}^{k} r_{\alpha-1,l-1}}.$$

Similarly, by (2.3), the RHS of (2.1) decreases by a fraction of

$$p(t_{new})\frac{r_{d,k-1}}{\sum_{l=1}^{k} r_{d,l-1}}.$$

Next we show that

$$\frac{r_{d,k-1}}{\sum_{l=1}^{k} r_{d,l-1}} \geq \frac{r_{\alpha-1,k-1}}{\sum_{l=1}^{k} r_{\alpha-1,l-1}}, \tag{2.4}$$

thus establishing the fact that (2.1) still holds on r'.

We prove (2.4) by induction. For the base case $k = 2$, by Property 2.2, we have

$$\frac{r_{d,1}}{r_{d,0} + r_{d,1}} = 1 - \frac{r_{d,0}}{r_{d,0} + r_{d,1}}$$

$$\geq 1 - \frac{r_{d,0}}{r_{d,0} + \frac{r_{\alpha-1,1}r_{d,0}}{r_{\alpha-1,0}}} = \frac{r_{\alpha-1,1}}{r_{\alpha-1,0} + r_{\alpha-1,1}}. \tag{2.5}$$

Next we consider $k + 1$ assuming (2.4) is true for k. Again by Property 2.2, we have

$$
\frac{r_{d,k}}{\sum_{l=1}^{k+1} r_{d,l-1}} \geq \frac{\frac{r_{\alpha-1,k} r_{d,k-1}}{r_{\alpha-1,k-1}}}{\sum_{l=1}^{k} r_{\alpha-1,l-1} \frac{r_{d,k-1}}{r_{\alpha-1,k-1}} + \frac{r_{\alpha-1,k} r_{d,k-1}}{r_{\alpha-1,k-1}}}
$$

$$
= \frac{r_{\alpha-1,k}}{\sum_{l=1}^{k+1} r_{\alpha-1,l-1}}. \tag{2.6}
$$

So (2.4) holds for all k, and the theorem is proved.   □

The way to maintain a compact set is simple if tuples are only inserted into D but never deleted. When a tuple t_{new} arrives, the first task is to compare its rank with t^d, the lowest ranked tuple in $C(D)$. If $t^d \prec_f t_{new}$, we simply discard t_{new} knowing that it will not affect the query results. Otherwise, we recompute the array r on $C(D) \cup \{t_{new}\}$, which gives us the updated compact set $C(D \cup \{t_{new}\})$ and also the updated top-k results.

Example 2.3. As shown in Example 2.1, the compact set for the dataset D in Table 2.1(a) is $C(D) = \{t^3, t^2, t^1\}$. We first consider a situation where a new tuple $t_{new} = 4$ arrives in D. The compact set remains unchanged because $t^1 \prec_f t_{new}$, i.e., $C(D \cup \{t_{new}\}) = C(D)$. Next, consider another tuple $t_{new} = 7$ arrives, which means that the compact set must be recomputed based on $C(D)$ and t_{new} because $t_{new} \prec_f t^1$. The confidence of t_{new} is a key factor for the new compact set. If the confidence is high, say, $p(t_{new}) = 0.9$, we have $C(D \cup \{t_{new}\}) = \{t^3, t_{new}, t^2\}$. If the confidence is low, say, $p(t_{new}) = 0.1$, we have $C(D \cup \{t_{new}\}) = \{t^3, t_{new}, t^2, t^1\}$.

However, the presence of expiring tuples makes the problem much more difficult, since if a tuple in $C(D)$ expires, this whole compact set becomes useless and we need to compute a new compact set from D. The main reason is that the array $r_{i,j}$ will change a lot when an entity in $C(D)$ fades out, making condition (2) of Definition 2.2 invalid. Thus, simply using one compact set does not allow us to discard any tuple in the window until it expires, using memory $\Omega(W)$. In the next section, we present our sliding-window synopses, which combine multiple compact sets together, so that we can safely discard most tuples in the window while still being able to maintain the up-to-date query results at any time as the window slides through time.

2.3   Four Synopses for Sliding Windows

The previous section shows that the compact set is self-maintainable under insertions. However, if a tuple in the compact set expires, then there is no way to reconstruct it without maintaining tuples outside the compact set. Then the question is, how many other tuples do we need to keep? This section will focus on answering this question.

First of all, notice that in the worst-case scenario, any tuple will be in the top-k result at some point in time as the window slides. In this case, any synopsis has to remember everything in the window in order to avoid incorrect query results. So, it is hopeless to design a synopsis with a sublinear worst-case space bound.

Example 2.4. Consider an uncertain stream where the value and the probability of the ith tuple t_i are both $\frac{1}{i}$. In this case, at any time point n, $n \geq W$, tuple t_{n-W+1} is in the query result of U-Top$k$, U-kRanks, and Pk-Top$k$. In this example, all tuples in the window must be saved.

However, examples like the one above seldom occur in practice. Therefore, we will assume that the tuples arrive in a random order and study the expected cost (both space and time) of the algorithms. This *random-order stream* model has received much attention lately from the streaming algorithms community [15,16,37], mainly because the worst-case bounds for many streaming problems are simply too pessimistic and thus meaningless. The random-order stream model has been argued to be a reasonable approximation of real-world data streams while often allowing for much better expected bounds. This model is an ideal choice for the study of our problem since as shown above, in the worst case, there is really nothing better one can do than the naive approach, which simply keeps all tuples in the sliding window.

Before presenting our solutions, we first analyze the direct adaptation of the existing technique to the sliding window setting, which we refer to as the *Base Synopsis*, or the *BS*. To make the analytical comparison with our synopses easier, we use H to denote the maximum size of the compact sets that are maintained in the synopsis. As argued in [41, 77], although in the worst case, $H = W$, but on most datasets, $H \ll W$. As discussed in the previous section, BS needs to keep all the W tuples in the window (in the rank order) and its compact set C. The array r takes $O(kH)$ space, thus the total space of BS is $O(W + kH)$, which is effectively $O(W)$ since $H \ll W$. When the window slides, if either the expiring tuple is in C, or the incoming tuple's rank is higher than the lowest ranked tuple in C, then we recompute C from all the tuples in the window. Since C keeps the highest-ranked tuples in the window, either event happens with probability $O(H/W)$, so the expected cost of maintaining C is $O(kH^2/W)$. Maintaining the tuples in the rank order takes $O(\log W)$ time per tuple. Thus the per-tuple processing cost is $O(kH^2/W + \log W)$.

In the following subsections, we present our sliding-window synopses. Each of them builds upon the previous one with new ideas, progressively improving either the space complexity or the processing time. Our final synopsis requires $O(H(k + \log W))$ space consumption and has a processing time of $O(kH^2/W + \log W)$. So it matches the processing time of BS while having a much lower space complexity. To appreciate this result, the reader is reminded that most streaming algorithms, e.g., most sketches [9, 64], require higher running times than the naive approach in order to achieve low space complexity.

Compact Set Queue. Our first synopsis, called the *Compact Set Queue (CSQ)*, is the simplest of all but forms the basis of more advanced synopses. Let S_i denote the set of the latest i tuples in the sliding window. In the CSQ, we simply keep all the distinct compact sets $C(S_i)$ for all $i = 1, \ldots, W$. We only keep the array r for $C(S_W)$ from which we can extract the top-k results. Since we have the compact set for each S_i, when a tuple in $C(S_W)$ expires, we can move $C(S_{W-1})$ forward to become the new $C(S_W)$.

Algorithm 1 MaintainCSQ

1: Tuple set $D \leftarrow \emptyset$; compact set queue $\Psi \leftarrow \emptyset$;
2: **for** each arriving tuple t **do**
3:     Insert t into D;
4:     **if** successfully create a compact set $C(D)$ for D **then**
5:         Append $C(D)$ to Ψ;
6:         Remove tuples in D older than t'' (including t''), where t'' is the oldest tuple in $C(D)$;
7:     **end if**
8:     **for** each compact set $C(S_i) \in \Psi$ from new to old **do**
9:         **if** $t \prec_f$ lowest ranked tuple in $C(S_i)$ **then**
10:            $C(S_i) \leftarrow C(C(S_i) \cup \{t\})$;
11:            Remove $C(S_i)$ from Ψ if $C(S_i) =$ the previous compact set in Ψ;
12:        **else**
13:            **break**;
14:        **end if**
15:     **end for**
16:     **if** the expiring tuple $\in C(S_W)$ **then**
17:         Remove $C(S_W)$ from Ψ;
18:         $C(S_W) \leftarrow$ first compact set in Ψ;
19:         Compute the array r on the new $C(S_W)$;
20:     **end if**
21: **end for**

Algorithm 1 describes the detailed algorithm to maintain the CSQ. We maintain a queue Ψ of all the distinct compact sets. The tuple set D temporarily keeps the newest tuples. Initially D does not admit a compact set. As tuples arrive at D, D will have a valid compact set at some point. When this happens, we create $C(D)$, and append it to Ψ. Tuples in D but older than the oldest tuple in $C(D)$ (including the oldest tuple in $C(D)$) are removed from D (lines 1–7). Note that after the removal, D does not admit a compact set anymore. Therefore, when D has collected enough new tuples, the new compact set it generates must be different from the existing

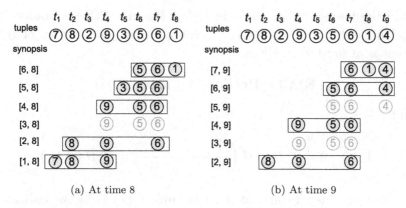

(a) At time 8   (b) At time 9

Fig. 2.1   Maintaining the CSQ

ones in Ψ. Next we update all the compact sets in Ψ in turn, while removing duplicates (lines 8–15). Finally, we check if the expiring tuple exists in $C(S_W)$, if so we remove $C(S_W)$ from Ψ, and the next compact set in Ψ becomes the new $C(S_W)$ (lines 16–20).

Example 2.5. Figure 2.1 shows how the CSQ evolves over time. For illustration purposes we assume $H = 3$ and all compact sets have exactly the three highest ranked tuples. Recall that H denotes the maximum size of the compact sets that are maintained in the synopsis. At time 8, the queue contains five compact sets, and $D = \{6, 1\}$, as shown in Figure 2.1(a). When tuple t_9 arrives, t_9 is inserted into D making $D = \{6, 1, 4\}$. Here, $C(D)$ exists and $C(D) = \{6, 1, 4\}$ is appended into the queue, with D reset to be $\{1, 4\}$. We then continue to check compact sets in the queue with t_9. The compact set for $S[5, 9]$ is removed from queue because it is same to the compact set for $S[6, 9]$. The oldest compact set in the queue is removed because of tuple expiring. Finally, there are four compact sets, as shown in Figure 2.1(b).

We then analyze the performance of CSQ. Let X_i be the indicator variable such that $X_i = 1$ if $C(S_i)$ is different from $C(S_{i+1})$, and $X_i = 0$ otherwise. It is obvious that the expected number of distinct compact sets in Ψ is $\mathbf{E}\left[\sum_{i=1}^{W} X_i\right]$. The event $C(S_{i+1}) \neq C(S_i)$ happens only when the rank of the oldest tuple in S_{i+1} is higher than the lowest ranked tuple in $C(S_i)$. Because $C(S_i)$ contains the $\leq H$ highest ranked tuples in S_i, the occurring probability of this event is at most H/i. Hence,

$$\mathbf{E}\left[X_i\right] = \mathbf{Pr}\left[X_i = 1\right] \leq \max\{1, H/i\}$$

and

$$\mathbf{E}\left[\sum_{i=1}^{W} X_i\right] \leq H + H\left(\frac{1}{H} + \cdots + \frac{1}{W}\right) = O(H \log W).$$

Now consider the arrival of a new tuple t. Let Y_i be the indicator variable such that $Y_i = 1$ iff $X_i = 1$ and t affects $C(S_{i+1})$. For the latter to happen, t must rank higher than the lowest ranked tuple in $C(S_{i+1})$, so $\mathbf{Pr}\left[Y_i = 1|X_i = 1\right] \leq \max\{1, H/(i+1)\}$. Hence, the expected number of compact sets affected by t is

$$\mathbf{E}\left[\sum_{i=1}^{W} Y_i\right] = \sum_{i=1}^{W} \mathbf{Pr}\left[X_i = 1\right] \mathbf{Pr}\left[Y_i = 1|X_i = 1\right]$$

$$\leq H + H^2\left(\frac{1}{H(H+1)} + \cdots + \frac{1}{W(W+1)}\right)$$

$$\leq H + H^2 \cdot \frac{1}{H} = O(H).$$

Hence, the expected number of distinct compact sets in CSQ is $O(H \log W)$; the expected number of compact sets that need to be updated per tuple is $O(H)$.

Since each compact set has size $O(H)$, and the array r has size $O(kH)$, the space bound is $O(H^2 \log W)$. Each compact set can be updated in time $O(kH)$ and there are $O(H)$ of them that need to be updated, so the total time for the update is $O(kH^2)$.

Compressed Compact Set Queue. Although CSQ only contains distinct compact sets, there is still a lot of redundancy as one tuple may appear in multiple compact sets. In the *Compressed Compact Set Queue (CCSQ)*, we try to eliminate this redundancy by only storing the difference between two adjacent compact sets $C(S_i)$ and $C(S_{i-1})$. More precisely, if $C(S_i) \neq C(S_{i-1})$, we keep both

$\Delta_i^+ = C(S_i) - C(S_{i-1})$ and $\Delta_i^- = C(S_{i-1}) - C(S_i)$. Now we can discard all the $C(S_i)$ in the queue Ψ except the newest one.

We need to bound the total size of these differences. First, since S_i has only one more tuple than S_{i-1}, it is clear that $|\Delta_i^+| \leq 1$. The total number of non-empty Δ_i^+ is $O(H \log W)$, so we have $\sum_{i=1}^{W} |\Delta_i^+| = O(H \log W)$. To bound the total size of all the Δ_i^-, we need the following property.

Example 2.6. Figure 2.2 shows how the CCSQ evolves over time. For illustration purposes we assume $H = 3$ and all compact sets have exactly the three highest ranked tuples. Recall that H denotes the maximum size of the compact sets that are maintained in the synopsis. At time 8, the latest compact set is $\{5, 6, 1\}$, and the difference of all adjacent compact sets is: $\{7, 8, 9, 3\}$, as shown in Figure 2.2(a). When tuple t_9 arrives, t_9 is inserted into D making $D = \{6, 1, 4\}$. Here, $C(D)$ exists and $C(D) = \{6, 1, 4\}$ becomes the latest compact set, with D reset to be $\{1, 4\}$. The difference of all adjacent compact sets now becomes $\{8, 9, 5\}$, as shown in Figure 2.2(b).

If tuple t appears both in $C(S_i)$ and $C(S_j)$, $i < j$, then it appears in all compact sets between $C(S_i)$ and $C(S_j)$, i.e., $t \in C(S_l)$ for all $i \leq l \leq j$. Thus, as we go from $C(S_1)$ to $C(S_W)$, once a tuple

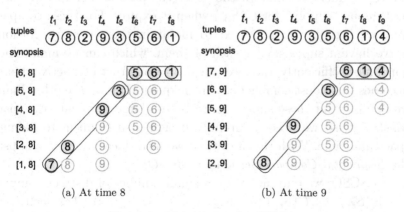

(a) At time 8   (b) At time 9

Fig. 2.2 Maintaining the CCSQ

disappears, it will never appear again. So, we have

$$\sum_{i=1}^{W} |\Delta_i^-| \le H + \sum_{i=1}^{W} |\Delta_i^+| = O(H \log W).$$

By this compression technique, we have reduced the space complexity of CSQ by roughly an $O(H)$ factor.

As argued above, storing all the compact sets with compression requires $O(H \log W)$ space. We also need the array r, which takes $O(kH)$ space. Hence, the space cost is $O(H(k + \log W))$. The processing time remains unchanged, since we can restore each $C(S_i)$ in Ψ by making a pass over Δ_i^+ and Δ_i^-, update it, and compute the new Δ_i^+ and Δ_i^-, all in time $O(kH^2)$.

Segmental Compact Set Queue. With CCSQ, we have lowered the space complexity of the synopsis to almost minimal: we only need one array r and keep $O(H \log W)$ tuples, as opposed to BS which stores all the W tuples. However, the maintenance cost of CCSQ is still very high. In the next two advanced synopses, we try to improve the processing time while maintaining the low space complexity.

We notice that the high computation complexity is due to the fact that $O(H)$ compact sets need to be updated per incoming tuple. However, only the oldest compact set $C(S_W)$ is needed to extract the top-k query results; all the other compact sets simply act as a continuous "supply" for $C(S_W)$ when it expires. For these compact sets, we actually do not need to maintain them exactly. As long as we have a super set for each of them, which can be maintained much more efficiently, then we can still reconstruct it exactly when it becomes the oldest compact set in the queue. But on the other hand, we do not want these super sets to be too large to violate the space constraint, so we need a carefully designed mechanism to balance space and time. With this intuition, we introduce our next synopsis, the *Segmental Compact Set Queue (SCSQ)*.

In SCSQ, we only maintain a small number of distinct compact sets $C(S_{\ell_1}), \ldots, C(S_{\ell_n})$, for $1 \le \ell_1 < \cdots < \ell_n \le W$. For each i, we also maintain Λ_{ℓ_i}, a set of tuples in $S_{\ell_{i+1}} - S_{\ell_i}$ (define $\ell_{n+1} = W$) such that $C(S_j) \subseteq S_{\ell_i} \cup \Lambda_{\ell_i}$ for all $\ell_i \leq j < \ell_{i+1}$. Note that any tuple in Λ_{ℓ_i} must rank higher than the lowest ranked tuple in $C(S_{\ell_i})$. Finally, we always keep $C(S_W)$ and its associated array r, from which we extract the top-k results. Especially, if $\forall \ell_i, |\Lambda_{\ell_i}| = 0$, then the SCSQ becomes a CSQ.

The main benefit of SCSQ is that it avoids generating too many compact sets, because tuples in Λ_{ℓ_i} are not used for refreshing the compact sets. On the other hand, in CCSQ, compressed compact sets must be *uncompressed* to deal with new tuples, which results in a high computation cost.

We maintain the following invariants in SCSQ throughout time[1]:

$$|\Lambda_{\ell_i}| \leq H, \quad \text{for } i = 1, \ldots, n; \tag{2.7}$$

$$|\Lambda_{\ell_i}| + |\Lambda_{\ell_{i+1}}| \geq H, \quad \text{for } i = 1, \ldots, n-1. \tag{2.8}$$

Whenever $C(S_W)$ expires, since the new compact set for the query q is a subset of $C(S_{\ell_n}) \cup \Lambda_{\ell_n}$, we can rebuild it in time $O(kH)$.

Whenever invariant Equation (2.8) is violated, we do a merge by setting $\Lambda_{\ell_i} := \Lambda_{\ell_i} \cup \Lambda_{\ell_{i+1}} \cup \{t'\}$, where t' is the oldest tuple in $C(S_{\ell_{i+1}})$, and then removing $C(S_{\ell_{i+1}}), \Lambda_{\ell_{i+1}}$. It is not difficult to verify that $\Lambda_{\ell_i} \cup C(S_{\ell_i})$ now contains all the tuples needed to cover any $C(S_j)$ for $\ell_i \leq j < \ell_{i+2}$, and both invariants Equations (2.7) and (2.8) are restored.

The procedure to maintain the SCSQ is shown in Algorithm 2, which is actually very similar to that of CSQ. The only difference is now we only update $C(S_W)$ and $C(S_{\ell_i})$ for each $i = 1, \ldots, n$. Next, if $C(S_{\ell_i})$ has changed, tuples in Λ_{ℓ_i} are simply removed if their ranks are lower than the lowest ranked tuple in $C(S_{\ell_i})$ (lines 9–10). Whenever invariant Equation (2.8) is violated, we do a merge as described above (line 11). Finally, if $C(S_W)$ expires, we compute a new $C(S_W)$ from $C(S_{\ell_n}) \cup \Lambda_{\ell_n}$.

---

[1]Note that H is not fixed in advance and may change over time. So, we update and use a new H whenever the maximum size of the compact sets currently maintained in the synopsis changes by a factor of 2. This does not affect the asymptotic bounds of our algorithms.

Algorithm 2 MaintainSCSQ

1: Segmental compact set queue $\Psi \leftarrow \emptyset$; Tuple set $D \leftarrow \emptyset$;
2: **for** each arriving tuple t **do**
3:      Insert t into D; remove expiring tuple in Ψ if possible;
4:      **if** successfully create a compact set $C(D)$ for D **then**
5:          Append a new segmental compact set Γ into Ψ, satisfying $\Gamma.\Lambda = \emptyset$, $\Gamma.C = C(D)$;
6:          Remove tuples in D older than $\texttt{old}(C(D))$ (including $\texttt{old}(C(D))$));
7:      **end if**
8:      **for** each segmental compact set $\Gamma' \in \Psi$ from new to old **do**
9:          Update $\Gamma'.C$ by: $\Gamma'.C \leftarrow C(\Gamma'.C \cup \{t\})$;
10:         Remove tuples in $\Gamma'.\Lambda$ if it $\succ_f$ lowest rank in $\Gamma'.C$;
11:         Merge with previous segmental compact set if violating invariant Equation 2.7- 2.8;
12:     **end for**
13:     **if** $C(S_W)$ is affected **then**
14:         Update $C(S_W)$;
15:     **end if**
16: **end for**

Example 2.7. Figure 2.3 shows how the SCSQ evolves over time. For illustration purposes we assume $H = 3$ and all compact sets have exactly the three highest ranked tuples. The queue contains two compact sets at time 8: $C(S_3) = \{5, 6, 1\}$, $\Lambda_3 = \emptyset$; $C(S_4) = \{3, 5, 6\}$, $\Lambda_4 = \{7, 8, 9\}$. When tuple t_9 arrives, the existing two compact sets are shifted and updated as $C(S_4) = \{5, 6, 4\}$, $C(S_5) = \{5, 6, 4\}$. At the same time, Λ_3 and Λ_4 are also shifted (but unchanged) to be Λ_4 and Λ_5. Since $C(S_4)$ and $C(S_5)$ are now the same, we delete $C(S_5)$, and set $\Lambda_4 = \Lambda_5$. A new compact set is created $C(S_3) = \{5, 6, 1\}$ and $\Lambda_3 = \emptyset$. Next, we remove the expiring tuple 8 from Λ_4. Since $|\Lambda_3| + |\Lambda_4| = 2 < H$, we do a merge, removing $C(S_4)$ while updating $\Lambda_3 := \Lambda_3 \cup \Lambda_4 \cup \{5\} = \{8, 9, 5\}$. Figure 2.3(b) shows the final status after tuple t_1 expires.

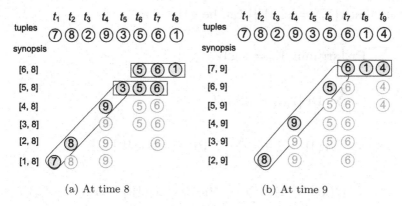

(a) At time 8   (b) At time 9

Fig. 2.3   Maintaining the SCSQ

We next show that SCSQ maintains expected $O(\log W)$ compact sets. Under the random-order stream model, all of $\ell_1, \ldots, \ell_n$, as well as n, are random variables. Below we show that $\mathbf{E}[n] = O(\log W)$.

Consider the stochastic process consisting of the sequence of random variables $\ell_1, \ell_3, \ell_5, \ldots$. We say that it is a good event if $\ell_{2i+1} \geq 2\ell_{2i-1}$, and a bad event otherwise. It is clear that the sequence will terminate before we have $\log W$ good events. We construct a sequence of indicator variables $X_1, X_2, \ldots$, where $X_i = 1$ iff the ith event is good, and let $Y_m = X_1 + \cdots + X_m$. Then $\mathbf{E}[n] \leq 2 \cdot \mathbf{E}[\arg\min_m\{Y_m = \log W\}]$.

Now we focus on bounding $\mathbf{E}[Y]$. Consider the bad event $\ell_{2i+1} < 2\ell_{2i-1}$. If this happens, due to invariant 2.8, there must be more than H tuples in $S_{2\ell_{2i-1}} - S_{\ell_{2i-1}}$ that rank higher than the Hth ranked tuple in $S_{\ell_{2i}}$. If so, among the top-$(2H)$ ranked tuples in $S_{2\ell_{2i-1}}$, more than half of them must be in the older half $S_{2\ell_{2i-1}} - S_{\ell_{2i-1}}$. This occurs with probability less than $1/2$. Therefore, for any i, the probability that the ith event is bad is less than $1/2$, or equivalently $\mathbf{Pr}[X_i = 1] > 1/2$.

Although $X_1, X_2, \ldots$ are not necessarily independent, the argument above holds for each X_i regardless of the values of X_j, $j \neq i$. Therefore, Y_m is *stochastically greater* than a binomial random variable $Z_m \sim \text{binomial}(m, 1/2)$: $Y_m \geq_{st} Z_m$. The expectation

$\mathbf{E}\left[\arg\min_m\{Y_m = \log W\}\right]$ can be written as

$$\sum_{i \geq 1} \mathbf{Pr}\left[\arg\min_m\{Y_m = \log W\} \geq i\right]$$

$$= \sum_{i \geq 1} \mathbf{Pr}\left[Y_{i-1} < \log W\right]$$

$$\leq 4\log W + 1 + \sum_{i \geq 4\log W} \mathbf{Pr}\left[Y_i < \log W\right]$$

$$\leq O(\log W) + \sum_{i \geq 4\log W} \mathbf{Pr}\left[Z_i < \log W\right] \quad (Y_m \geq_{st} Z_m)$$

$$\leq O(\log W) + \sum_{i \geq 4\log W} e^{-(i/2 - \log W)^2/i} \quad \text{(Chernoff bound)}$$

$$\leq O(\log W) + \sum_{i \geq 4\log W} e^{-i/16} = O(\log W).$$

Since the array r has size $O(kH)$ and each compact set has size $O(H)$, the space bound of SCSQ is $O(H(k + \log W))$. Updating all the compact sets takes $O(kH \log W)$ time. Updating all the Λ_{ℓ_i} and doing the necessary merges take time $O(H \log W)$, hence the per-tuple time cost is $O(kH \log W)$.

SCSQ with Buffering. SCSQ makes an $O(H)$-factor improvement over the previous synopses in terms of processing time, but there is still room for improvement. With our final synopsis, *SCSQ-Buffer*, we make another significant improvement by augmenting SCSQ with a buffering technique, reducing the processing time to minimum.

The basic intuition here is that since only $C(S_W)$ is useful for the query, we update only this compact set every time the window slides. For the rest of the compact sets, we update them in batches. More precisely, we keep a buffer B of size kH for the latest tuples.[2] (We assume $W > kH$; otherwise we just switch to BS.) When the buffer

---

[2]We change the size of the buffer whenever H changes by a factor of 2. See also Footnote 1.

is full, we empty it and make necessary changes to the synopsis. The detailed algorithm is shown in Algorithm 3.

Algorithm 3 maintainSCSQ-buffer

1: Let B be a buffer with size kH;
2: **for** each arriving tuple t **do**
3:   Insert t into B;
4:   **if** B is full **then**
5:     Find the smallest i such that B_i admits a compact set;
6:     Starting from i, build SCSQ on B;
7:     Update the existing SCSQ;
8:     $B \leftarrow \emptyset$;
9:   **end if**
10:   **if** $C(S_W)$ is affected **then**
11:     Update $C(S_W)$;
12:   **end if**
13:   Remove expired compact sets in SCSQ;
14: **end for**

First, we need to build new compact sets and the relevant Λ_ℓ's for the tuples in B. Let B_i be the set of i latest tuples in B. To do so, we first do a binary search to find the smallest i such that B_i admits a compact set (line 5). Since checking each B_i takes $O(kH)$ time, the binary search takes $O(kH \log(kH))$ time. Then we build the first compact set. Next we scan the remaining tuples from new to old, putting into Λ_i those tuples ranking higher than the lowest ranked one in $C(B_i)$. When $|\Lambda_i| = H$ we stop, and restart the same process by building another compact set. We will build $O(\log(kH))$ new compact sets for B, spending $O(kH \log(kH))$ time in total (line 6).

Secondly, we update all the existing compact sets $C(S_{\ell_i})$ and the Λ_{ℓ_i} with all the tuples in B (line 7). Since there are $O(\log W)$ compact sets and updating each one takes $O(kH)$ time, the total cost is $O(kH \log W)$. Updating all the Λ_{ℓ_i} and making all the necessary merges take $O(H \log W)$ time. Therefore, the total cost for emptying a buffer of size kH is $O(kH \log(kH) + kH \log W) = O(kH \log W)$. So, the amortized cost per tuple is only $O(\log W)$.

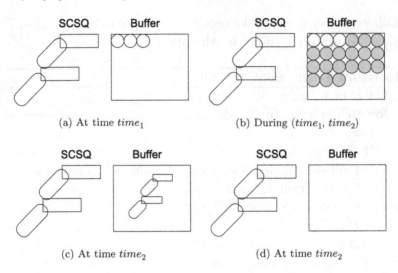

(a) At time $time_1$ (b) During $(time_1, time_2)$

(c) At time $time_2$ (d) At time $time_2$

Fig. 2.4   Maintaining the SCSQ-buffer

Finally, for each incoming tuple, we always update $C(S_W)$ if necessary (line 10–12). Similar to the case with BS, $C(S_W)$ is affected with probability $O(H/W)$, so the cost of maintaining $C(S_W)$ is $O(kH^2/W)$.

Example 2.8. Figure 2.4 demonstrates how Algorithm 3 runs with arriving tuples. A buffer is used to store the new tuples, and a SCSQ is built for the tuples in the sliding window except the buffered tuples. At time $time_1$, the buffer is partly filled (Figure 2.4(a)). During the time interval $(time_1, time_2)$, arriving tuples are inserted into the buffer until the buffer is full, while the SCSQ is nearly unchanged: only the expiring tuples or compact sets are removed from it (Figure 2.4(b)). When the buffer is full at time $time_2$, a new SCSQ is constructed for the buffered tuples. Afterward, this newly generated SCSQ is merged with the original SCSQ, and the buffer is emptied (Figures 2.4(c) and 2.4(d)).

The space consumption of SCSQ-buffer methods mainly consists of two aspects: the SCSQ and the buffer. The SCSQ consumes $O(H(k + \log W))$, and the buffer takes $O(kH)$, so the total space consumption is $O(H(k + \log W))$.

The processing cost of Algorithm maintain SCSQ-buffer consists of two parts. Part I: processing when the buffer B is full. Part II: updating $C(S_W)$ when $C(S_W)$ is affected.

At Part I, the first task is to do a binary search to find the smallest i such that B_i admits a compact set (line 5). Since checking each B_i takes $O(kH)$ time, the binary search takes $O(kH \log(kH))$ time. The second task is to scan the remaining tuples from new to old to build SCSQ on B (line 6). As analyzed above, we will build $O(\log(kH))$ new compact sets for B, spending $O(kH \log(kH))$ time in total. The last task is to update existing SCSQ with all the tuples in B (line 7). Since there are $O(\log W)$ compact sets and updating each one takes $O(kH)$ time, the total cost is $O(kH \log W)$. Updating all the affiliated tuples and making all the necessary merges take $O(H \log W)$ time. Therefore, the total cost for emptying a buffer of size kH is $O(kH \log(kH) + kH \log(kH) + kH \log W + H \log W) = O(kH \log W)$. So, the amortized cost per tuple is only $O(\log W)$.

At part II, we update $C(S_W)$ if it is affected (lines 10–12). The probability of this event is $O(H/W)$, and updating the $C(S_W)$ costs $O(kH)$, so the cost of maintaining $C(S_W)$ is $O(kH^2/W)$.

Finally, the amortized processing time is: $O(kH^2/W + \log W)$.

We summarize the space and time complexities of all five synopses we have presented so far in Table 2.3. Recall that H represents the maximum size of compact sets during executing, which is mainly affected by two factors, inclusive of parameter k that is fixed in advance and the average confidence of high-ranked tuples

Table 2.3 Asymptotic Space and Processing Time Bounds Analysis

	Space	Processing time
BS	$O(W + kH)$	$O(kH^2/W + \log W)$
CSQ	$O(H^2 \log W)$	$O(kH^2)$
CCSQ	$O(H(k + \log W))$	$O(kH^2)$
SCSQ	$O(H(k + \log W))$	$O(kH \log W)$
SCSQ-Buffer	$O(H(k + \log W))$	$O(kH^2/W + \log W)$

in a stream segment. In general, smaller average confidence leads to greater H. For a random-order stream, the situation that lots of high-ranked tuples with low confidence in a stream segment almost never happens. So, bearing in mind that $k < H \ll W$, we can see that SCSQ-Buffer has both the best space bound and the best processing time.

2.4 Supporting Other Top-k Definitions

As we have seen, our synopses are quite general in the sense that other top-k query definitions can be plugged into the framework if a compact set can be defined with sufficiency and self-maintenance with respect to insertions. This section briefly shows how to support the other three top-k definitions on uncertain data proposed in the literature in our framework. In fact, all the existing solutions read the tuples in the rank order, and stop as soon as the correctness of the result is guaranteed. Such an approach naturally yields a compact set which is also sufficient. So, we only need to prove self-maintainability.

PT-k queries [41]. Its *compact set* $C(D)$ with a threshold τ on an uncertain dataset D is the smallest subset of D that satisfies the following conditions. (1) $\forall t' \in C(D)$ and $t'' \in D - C(D)$, $t' \prec_f t''$. (2) $\tau \geq \sum_{1 \leq l \leq k} r_{d,l-1}$, where d is the size of $C(D)$.

U-kRanks queries [77]. Its *compact set* $C(D)$ on an uncertain dataset D is the smallest subset of D that satisfies the following conditions. (1) $\forall t' \in C(D)$ and $t'' \in D - C(D)$, $t' \prec_f t''$. (2) Let d be the size of $C(D)$, then

$$\max_{1 \leq i \leq d} p(t^i) r_{i-1,j-1} \geq \max_{1 \leq l \leq k} r_{d,l-1}, \quad \text{for } j = 1, \ldots, k. \tag{2.9}$$

As defined, the self-maintainability of condition Equation (2.9) is unwieldy to prove, so we first convert it to an equivalent, but much simpler condition. Specifically, we replace Equation (2.9) with the following:

$$p(t^\alpha) r_{\alpha-1,k-1} \geq \max_{1 \leq l \leq k} r_{d,l-1}, \quad \text{for some } \alpha \leq d. \tag{2.10}$$

U-Top$k$ queries [77]. Its *compact set* $C(D)$ on an uncertain dataset D is $C(D) = D_d$ where d is the smallest such that

$$\max_{k \leq i \leq d} \rho_i \geq \prod_{1 \leq i \leq d} \max\{p(t^i), 1 - p(t^i)\}. \tag{2.11}$$

We define the symbol ρ_i below. Suppose the tuples in D are $t^1, t^2, \ldots$ in the decreasing rank order. Consider a k-vector $T = (t^{m_1}, \ldots, t^{m_k})$. Let $\mathbf{Pr}\,[T]$ be the probability of T being the top-k tuples in a random possible world. We have

$$\mathbf{Pr}\,[T] = \prod_{i=1}^{k} p(t^{m_i}) \prod_{i < m_k, t^i \notin T} (1 - p(t^i)). \tag{2.12}$$

Recall that a U-Top$k$ query returns the vector T with maximum $\mathbf{Pr}\,[T]$. Let $D_i = \{t_1, \ldots, t_i\}$, and let D_i^p be the subset of D_i containing the k tuples with maximal probabilities in D_i. Define ρ_i as

$$\rho_i = \prod_{t^j \in D_i^p} p(t^j) \prod_{j \leq d, t_j \notin D_i^p} (1 - p(t^j)). \tag{2.13}$$

2.5 Experimental Results

In this section, we present an experimental study with both synthetic and real data to compare the five algorithms discussed so far, namely, BS, CSQ, CCSQ, SCSQ, and SCSQ-Buffer. All the algorithms are implemented in C and the experiments are performed on an openSUSE system with Intel Core 2 CPU (2.4GHz) and 4G memory.

Results on synthetic data. We created a synthetic dataset containing 20 million tuples. The rank of each tuple t is randomly generated from 1 to 20 million without replacement and the probability $p(t)$ is uniformly distributed in $(0, 1)$.

Figure 2.5 shows the number of tuples in the compact set for the Pk-top$k$ query for this dataset, as k increases. We can see that it is quite small and basically linear in k. This justifies our assumption that H is usually much smaller than the size of the dataset. Note

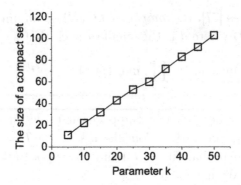

Fig. 2.5   Size of the compact set

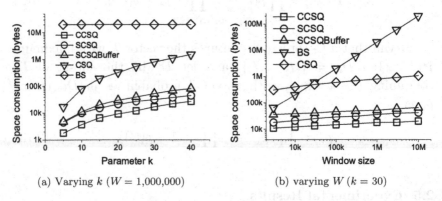

(a) Varying k ($W = 1,000,000$)   (b) varying W ($k = 30$)

Fig. 2.6   Space consumption on synthetic dataset

that the previous studies [41, 77] also observed similar behaviors on the size of the compact set.

Next, we feed the dataset in a streaming fashion to each of the synopses and measure their space consumption and processing time. Figure 2.6 shows the space consumption of the synopses with varying k and varying window size W, respectively. For simplicity, when calculating the space consumption we only counted the tuples and the array r, assuming that each tuple takes 10 bytes and each array entry takes 4 bytes. Keep in mind that, in real applications, the tuples could be much larger as it may contain multiple attributes including long fields like texts. So the sizes for the synopses shown here are only for comparison purposes; the actual sizes will be much larger and application-dependent. The experimental results agree with our theoretical bounds in Table 2.3 very well: BS is the largest, and its size is dominated by the window size W, irrespective to k. CSQ reduces the size considerably compared with BS, except for very small window sizes. All the other synopses are basically comparable in terms of size, all of which are significantly smaller than CSQ and BS. In general, we observe a space reduction of 2 to 3 orders of magnitude from BS to CCSQ and SCSQ/SCSQ-Buffer on large window sizes.

Figure 2.7 shows the per-tuple processing cost of the five methods. We can observe that CSQ and CCSQ runs slowest,

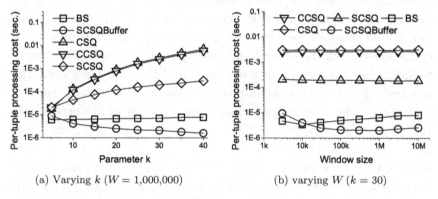

(a) Varying k ($W = 1,000,000$)   (b) varying W ($k = 30$)

Fig. 2.7 Per-tuple cost on synthetic dataset

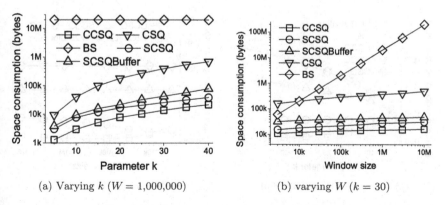

(a) Varying k ($W = 1,000,000$)   (b) varying W ($k = 30$)

Fig. 2.8 Space consumption on real dataset

due to their cubic dependency on k (since H is roughly linear in k). SCSQ is better, since the dependency on k is quadratic. BS and SCSQ-Buffer run the fastest. Interestingly, although they have the same asymptotic bound, we observe that SCSQ-Buffer actually runs even faster than BS. This is a bit counter-intuitive since what BS does for each tuple is very simple. It maintains all the tuples in the window in sorted order (using two balanced binary tree), and simply inserts and deletes tuples in this tree as they arrive and expire. In addition, it rebuilds $C(S_W)$ if it becomes invalid. The latter step is also done in SCSQ-Buffer. The explanation is that although maintaining a balanced binary tree is computationally easy, it is quite memory intensive. When we perform an insertion or a deletion, many nodes in the tree, possibly in different memory locations, are read and written, causing a lot of cache misses. On the other hand, SCSQ-Buffer is much more cache friendly, due to its small memory print and the way it performs the batched updates. Another interesting observation is that the per-tuple processing cost either remains the same or even decreases as the window size increases. The reason is that an incoming tuple has a smaller probability to affect the existing compact sets when the window size is larger, thus saving the computation cost. Similar phenomenon can also be observed in Figures 2.9(b), 2.10(d), 2.11(d), and 2.12(d).

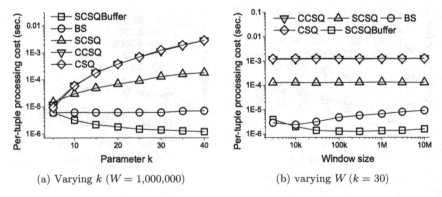

(a) Varying k ($W = 1,000,000$)   (b) varying W ($k = 30$)

Fig. 2.9   Per-tuple processing cost on real dataset

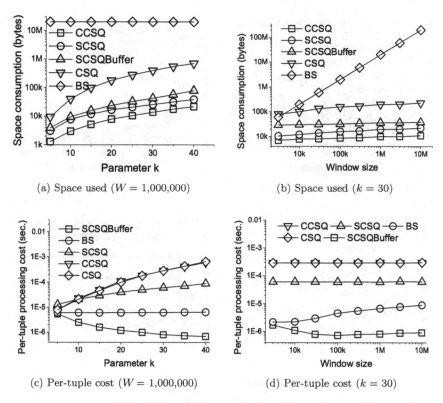

(a) Space used (W = 1,000,000)

(b) Space used (k = 30)

(c) Per-tuple cost (W = 1,000,000)

(d) Per-tuple cost (k = 30)

Fig. 2.10   PT-k query on real dataset

Results on real data. We used the International Ice Patrol (IIP) Iceberg Sightings Database[3] to examine the efficiency of our synopses in real applications. The IIP Iceberg Sightings Database collects information on iceberg activity in North Atlantic to monitor iceberg danger near the Grand Banks of Newfoundland by sighting icebergs, plotting and predicting iceberg drift, and broadcasting all known icebergs to prevent icebergs threatening. In the database, each sighting record contains the date, location, shape, size, number of days drifted, etc. It is crucial to find the icebergs drifting for long periods, so use the number of days drifted as the ranking attribute. Each sighting record in the database contains a confidence level

---

[3]http://nsidc.org/data/g00807.html.

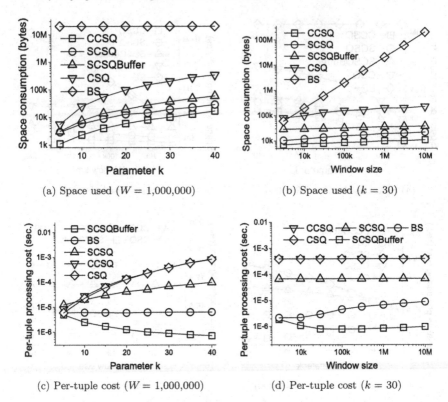

(a) Space used ($W = 1,000,000$)   (b) Space used ($k = 30$)

(c) Per-tuple cost ($W = 1,000,000$)   (d) Per-tuple cost ($k = 30$)

Fig. 2.11 U-kRanks query on real dataset

attribute according to the source of sighting, including R/V (radar and visual), VIS (visual only), RAD (radar only), SAT-LOW (low earth orbit satellite), SAT-MED (medium earth orbit satellite), SAT-HIGH (high earth orbit satellite), and EST (estimated, used before 2005). We gathered all of records from 1998 to 2007 and resulted in 44,440 records.

UncertainIIP. Based on the IIP dataset mentioned above, we created a 20,000,000-record data stream by repeatedly selecting records randomly. We converted these six confidence levels to probabilities 0.8, 0.7, 0.6, 0.5, 0.4, 0.3, and 0.4 respectively.

The experimental results on this real dataset are shown in Figures 2.8 and 2.9. We observe very similar results as those on the synthetic data, which demonstrates the robustness of our synopses.

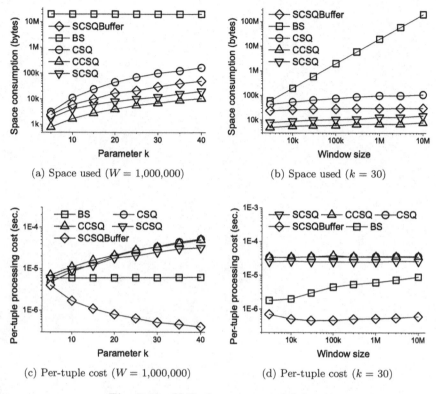

(a) Space used ($W = 1,000,000$)

(b) Space used ($k = 30$)

(c) Per-tuple cost ($W = 1,000,000$)

(d) Per-tuple cost ($k = 30$)

Fig. 2.12   U-Top$k$ query on real dataset

Other top-k queries. We also implemented the compact sets for the other three top-k definitions: PT-k, U-kRanks, and U-Top$k$. We plugged them into our synopses and conducted experiments on the real dataset. The results are shown in Figures 2.10, 2.11, and 2.12. Again, both the space consumption and processing time have very similar behaviors as those on the Pk-top$k$ query, which testifies the generality of our framework.

Chapter 3

ER-Top*k* Query Over the Landmark Model

3.1 Problem Definition

Let D denote a discrete base domain, and $\perp$ a special symbol representing a value out of D. Let S be an uncertain data stream, $S = \{t_1, t_2, \ldots, t_N\}$. The ith tuple in the stream, t_i, is described as $\langle (v_{i,1}, p_{i,1}), \ldots, (v_{i,s_i}, p_{i,s_i}) \rangle$. For each $l, 1 \leq l \leq s_i$, we have: $v_{i,l} \in D$ and $p_{i,l} \in (0, 1]$. $\sum_{l=1}^{s_i} p_{i,l} \leq 1$. For simplicity, we also assume $v_{i,1} < v_{i,2} < \cdots < v_{i,i_s}$.

Definition 3.1 (Expected Rank Top-*k*, ER-Top*k* in abbr.). [22] The ER-Top*k* query returns k tuples with the smallest values of $r(t)$, where $r(t) = \sum_{pw \in PW} \mathbf{Pr}\,[pw] \cdot rank_{pw}(t)$, PW is the possible world space, $\mathbf{Pr}\,[pw]$ is the probability of a possible world instance pw, and $rank_{pw}(t)$ returns the rank of t in pw, i.e., it returns the number of tuples ranked higher than t if $t \in pw$, or the number of tuples in pw ($|pw|$) otherwise.

By definition and linearity of expectation, the *expected rank* of tuple t_i, $r(t_i)$, is computed as follows:

$$
r(t_i) = \sum_{l=1}^{s_i} p_{i,l}(q(v_{i,l}) - q_i(v_{i,l}))
$$

$$
+ \left(1 - \sum_{l=1}^{s_i} p_{i,l}\right) \left(E[|pw|] - \sum_{l=1}^{s_i} p_{i,l}\right), \qquad (3.1)
$$

43

where $q(v)$ is the sum of the probabilities of all tuples greater than v, and $q_i(v)$ is the sum of the probabilities of tuple t_i greater than v, i.e., $q_i(v) = \sum_{l, v_{i,l} > v} p_{i,l}$, and $q(v) = \sum_i q_i(v)$. Let $|pw|$ denote the number of tuples in the possible world pw, so that $E[|pw|] = \sum_{i,l} p_{i,l}$.

Example 3.1. Consider the dataset in Table 1.1. The expected size of all possible worlds $E[|pw|] = \sum_{i,l} p_{i,l} = 3.3$. $r(t_1) = 0.6 \times ((1.0 + 0.4 + 0.4) - 0.4) + 0.4 \times (0.4 - 0) = 1.0$, $r(t_3) = 0.4 \times 0 + (1 - 0.4) \times (3.3 - 0.4) = 1.74$. Similarly, $r(t_2) = 0.8$, $r(t_4) = 2.4$. So, the ER-Top$k$ query returns $\{t_2, t_1\}$ when $k = 2$.

Definition 3.2 (Threshold Top$k$ query, TTk(S, τ) in abbr.). A *TTk* query returns all tuples (say, t_i) in the stream S satisfying $r_i(t_i) \leq \tau$, where $r_i(t_i)$ is the rank of t_i at time i, and τ is a threshold.

According to Equation (3.1), computing $r_i(t_i)$ requires full information of $q(v)$ since we know nothing about t_i until it arrives. Hence, the space cost of an arbitrary algorithm is $O(Z)$, where Z is the number of distinct values in $S[1..i]$. The space cost becomes huge when Z continues to grow, so that it is necessary to devise an approximate solution with succinct space consumption.

Definition 3.3 (approximate Threshold Top$k$ query, aTTk $(S, \tau, \epsilon, \delta)$ in abbr.). Given an error parameter ϵ and a probability parameter δ, $0 \leq \epsilon, \delta \leq 1$, an *aTTk* query returns all tuples (say, t_i) in the stream S satisfying $\hat{r}_i(t_i) \leq \tau$, where τ is a threshold, $\hat{r}_i(t_i)$ is an estimate of $r_i(t_i)$, and $\frac{|\hat{r}_i(t_i) - r_i(t_i)|}{r_i(t_i)} \leq \epsilon$ with confidence at least $1 - \delta$.

Example 3.2. Consider a small data stream of four tuples in Table 1.1. For the first tuple t_1, $r_1(t_1) = 0$. When the next tuple t_2 arrives, $r_2(t_2)$ is computed as $r_2(t_2) = 0.6$, because $q(60) = 0.6$ and $q_2(60) = 0$. Similarly, we have $r_3(t_3) = 0.8$, $r_4(t_4) = 2.0$. So, $TTk(S, 0.7)$ returns t_1 and t_2. Assume an approximate method estimates the values of $r_1(t_1), \ldots, r_4(t_4)$ as 0, 0.72, 0.65 and 2.3 respectively when $\epsilon = 0.5$ and $\delta = 0.1$ in one run. Then, $aTTk(S, 0.7, 0.5, 0.1)$ returns t_1 and t_3.

3.2 Handling ER-Top$k$

According to Equation (3.1), the expected rank may change with time going on since the function $q(v)$ is based on all tuples till now. For example, at time 4, $r(t_2) = 0.8$, $r(t_1) = 1.0$, $r(t_2) < r(t_1)$ (in Example 3.1). Assume the next tuple t_5 is $\langle(65, 1.0)\rangle$. Then, $r(t_1) = 1.6$, and $r(t_2) = 1.8$. It implies that $r(t_i) > r(t_j)$ at some time point does not mean $r(t_i) > r(t_j)$ forever.

Fortunately, we actually find some pairs of tuples, t_i and t_j, such that $r(t_i) > r(t_j)$ or $r(t_j) < r(t_i)$ always holds. For convenience, we use $t_i \prec t_j$ to denote the situation where $r(t_i) < r(t_j)$ holds forever, and $t_i \succ t_j$ vice versa. For convenience, we claim t_i *dominates* t_j if $t_i \prec t_j$, or t_i is *dominated* by t_j if $t_i \succ t_j$. For any two tuples t_i and t_j, $t_i \prec t_j$ only when (i) $\forall v$, $q_i(v) \geq q_j(v)$, and (ii) $\exists v$, $q_i(v) > q_j(v)$. Remember that $q_i(v) = \sum_{l, v_{i,l} > v} p_{i,l}$.

Example 3.3. Figure 3.1 illustrates the functions $q_i(v)$ for all tuples in Table 1.1. Obviously, $t_1 \prec t_4$, $t_2 \prec t_4$. For two tuples t_1 and t_2, neither $t_1 \prec t_2$ nor $t_2 \prec t_1$ holds.

A tuple t cannot belong to the query result if there exist at least k tuples (say, t'), $t' \prec t$. We then check whether a tuple may be output in the future or not. Such candidate tuples must be stored in the system.

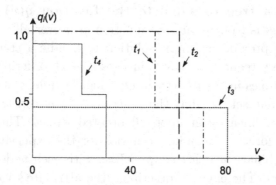

Fig. 3.1 The functions $q_i(v)$, for each $1 \leq i \leq 4$

Algorithm 4 processStream()

1: Empty a domGraph G and a probTree T;

2: **for** each arriving tuple t **do**

3:     Invoke Algorithm 5 (maintainProbTree(t, T));

4:     Invoke Algorithm 7 (maintainDomGraph(t, G));

5: **end for**

Note that a tuple cannot belong to the query result even if it is not dominated by k tuples under some situations. See the example below.

Example 3.4. Let us consider a situation, $k = 1$. There are three tuples, $t_1 = \langle (9, 0.6), (8, 0.2), (7, 0.1), (6, 0.1) \rangle$, $t_2 = \langle (11, 0.4), (6, 0.5), (5, 0.1) \rangle$, $t_3 = \langle (10, 0.1), (9, 0.4), (4, 0.5) \rangle$. No tuple dominates another tuple. But the tuple t_3 will not be output since its expected rank $r(t_3)$ will be greater than t_1 or t_2 no matter what tuples come later. In other words, $r(t_1) + r(t_2) - 2r(t_3) < 0$ always holds since $q(\cdot)$ is monotonous (Equation (3.1)).

However, discovering all candidate tuples like Example 3.4 is quite expensive since it needs to check a huge number of tuples. Consequently, we only store a small number of candidate tuples. Algorithm 4 is the main framework of our exact solution, which invokes `maintainProbTree` and `maintainDomGraph` repeatedly to maintain two structures, *probTree* and *domGraph*.

probTree: a tree to simulate the function $q(v)$. An indispensable task is to maintain the function $q(v)$ over all tuples in the stream. [22] provides a simple solution to handle a static dataset. When a query request arrives, it invokes a quick ordering algorithm to sort all tuples in the dataset in $O(N \log N)$ time, where N is the size of the dataset, so that the function $q(v)$ is constructed after conducting a linear scan upon all ordered tuples. This approach cannot suit for the streaming scenarios for the expensive cost. We construct a binary search tree, *probTree*, with each node in form of (v, p, l, r, par). The entry v, describing the attribute's value, is also the *key* of the tree. The entry p represents the probability sum of

---

Algorithm 5 maintainProbTree(t, T)

1: **for** each entry (v_j, p_j) in a tuple t **do**
2:   $w \leftarrow T.root$;
3:   Update $T.root \leftarrow \text{new} Node(v_j, p_j)$, and goto Line 1 if T is empty (i.e., $w = NULL$);
4:   **while** $w \neq NULL$ **do**
5:     **if** $w.v > v_j$ **then**
6:       If $w.l \neq NULL$, set $w \leftarrow w.l$; otherwise, $w.l \leftarrow \text{newNode}(v_j, p_j)$, and goto Line 4;
7:     **else if** $w.v < v_j$ **then**
8:       $w.p \leftarrow w.p + p_j$;
9:       If $w.r \neq NULL$, set $w \leftarrow w.r$; otherwise, $w.r \leftarrow \text{newNode}(v_j, p_j)$, and goto Line 4;
10:    **else**
11:      $w.p \leftarrow w.p + p_j$; goto Line 4;
12:    **end if**
13:   **end while**
14: **end for**

---

some tuples. The rest three entries, l, r and *par*, are the references to its left child, right child and parent nodes respectively.

Algorithm `maintainProbTree` (Algorithm 5) describes how to maintain a *probTree* T continuously when a new tuple $t = \langle (v_1, p_1), \ldots, (v_{s_t}, p_{s_t}) \rangle$ arrives. Initially, we insert a new node of t into T as the root node if T is empty. In general, the algorithm begins to seek a target node with a *key* (or equally the entry v) equal to v_j. If such node is found, its entry p increases by p_j. Otherwise, we insert a new node of (v_j, p_j) into T. Moreover, for each node w along the path from *root* to the destination (a node with entry v equal to v_j), the entry p is updated as $w.p \leftarrow w.p + p_j$ if $w.v < v_j$.

Algorithm `getq` (Algorithm 6) describes how to compute $q(v)$ by a probTree T. It visits some nodes along the path from the *root* node to a destination node with v equal to $\min_{w \in T, w.v > v}(w.v)$. The variable *sum*, representing the result value, is initialized to zero at

---

Algorithm 6 getq(v, T)

1: $sum \leftarrow 0$; $w \leftarrow T.root$;
2: **while** $w \neq NULL$ **do**
3: **if** $w.v > v$ **then**
4:    $sum \leftarrow sum + w.p$; $w \leftarrow w.l$;
5: **else**
6:    $w \leftarrow w.r$;
7: **end if**
8: **end while**
9: **return** sum;

---

first. For any node w in the path, sum is updated as $sum \leftarrow sum + w.p$ if $w.v > v$.

The correctness of Algorithm 6 comes from the construction of a *probTree*. Let $(v_{i,l}, p_{i,l})$ be an arbitrary attribute–probability pair in the data stream S. Let $RT(w)$ denote a sub-tree containing w and all nodes in its right sub-tree. For each node w in the *probTree*, p is the sum of the probabilities of all attribute-probability pairs with keys at its right side, i.e., $w.p = \sum_{v_{i,l} \in RT(w)} p_{i,l}$. Once it visits a node w such that $w.v > v$, it will visit the left child; otherwise, it will visit the right child (lines 3–7).

Example 3.5. Figure 3.3 illustrates the probTree at time 5 and 6 respectively. Each node is affiliated with information (v, p). When tuple t_6 $\langle (10, 0.4), (5, 0.6) \rangle$ arrives, it finds node n_3 since $n_3.v = 10$, following which $n_3.p$ is updated to 1.1 ($= 0.7 + 0.4$). Since $n_1.v = 9 < 10$ holds where n_1 is the parent node of n_3, its entry $n_1.p$ is also

Tuple	Attribute Value
t_1	$\langle (9, 0.3), (7, 0.7) \rangle$
t_2	$\langle (10, 0.4), (8, 0.6) \rangle$
t_3	$\langle (7, 1.0) \rangle$
t_4	$\langle (9, 0.5), (8, 0.4), (7, 0.1) \rangle$
t_5	$\langle (11, 0.3), (4, 0.7) \rangle$
t_6	$\langle (10, 0.4), (5, 0.6) \rangle$

Fig. 3.2 A small dataset

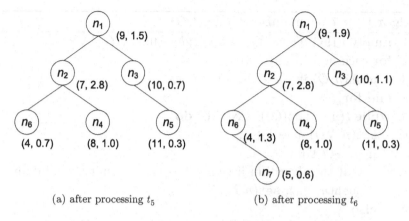

(a) after processing t_5 (b) after processing t_6

Fig. 3.3 An example of probTree upon Figure 3.2

updated to 1.9 ($= 1.5 + 0.4$). Subsequently, it inserts a new node n_7 of pair $(5, 0.6)$ into the *probTree* since there is no node with $v = 5$ now. Similarly, $n_6.p$ is updated to 1.3 ($= 0.7 + 0.6$) since $n_6.v < n_7.v$.

It is convenient to compute $q(v)$ based on a *probTree*. Assume $v = 8$. At first, it visits the *root* node n_1 to set *sum* to 1.9 since $n_1.v = 9 > 8$. Next, it visits the left node, n_2, and does nothing since $n_2.v = 7 < 8$. Subsequently, it visits the right node, n_4, and finds $n_4.v = 8$. Finally, it returns 1.9.

Assume the tuples in the stream arrive out of order. Let N denote the size of the data stream, s denote the maximum probability option, i.e., $s = \max_{i=1}^{N} s_i$. Obviously, the size of a *probTree* is $O(sN)$. The cost on inserting a tuple or computing $q(\cdot)$ is dependent on the height of the probTree. When each item is inserted in order, the height is $O(sN)$ under the worst case. Otherwise, the expected height of a randomly built binary search tree on sN keys is $O(\log(sN))$ [19]. Then, the amortized cost on inserting a tuple is $O(s\log(sN))$, and the cost on computing $q(\cdot)$ is $O(\log(sN))$.

domGraph: a graph to store candidate tuples. *DomGraph* is a graph to store all candidate tuples. Each node is described in form of $(t, T_{\prec}, T_{\succ}, state, c)$. The entry t refers to a tuple in the stream. $T_{\prec}$ represents a set of tuples with rank just higher than t, i.e., (i) $\forall t' \in T_{\prec}, t' \prec t$, and (ii) $\nexists t', t'' \in T_{\prec}$ such that $t' \prec t''$. $T_{\succ}$ represents a

---

Algorithm 7 maintainDomGraph(t, G)

1: Empty FIFO queues Q, $Q_{\prec}$, $Q_{\succ}$; $b \leftarrow 0$; set($G,$ TV);
2: **for** each node n in G **do**
3:     push(n, Q) if $\nexists n' \in G$, $n.t \prec n'.t$;
4: **end for**
5: **while** (($n \leftarrow$ pop(Q)) $\neq$ NULL) **do**
6:     set($n,$ VD); $b \leftarrow b + 1$;
7:     **if** $n.t \prec t$ **then**
8:         Exit the algorithm if ($n.c \geq k - 1$); // t isn't a candidate
9:         push($n, Q_{\prec}$); set($n.T_{\prec},$ NV);
10:     **else**
11:         push($n, Q_{\succ}$) and $Q_{\succ} \leftarrow Q_{\succ} - n.T_{\succ}$ if $t \prec n.t$;
12:         pushDominated(n, Q);
13:     **end if**
14: **end while**
15: Create a new node $n_{new}(t, Q_{\prec}, Q_{\succ}, |G| + |Q_{\prec}| - b,$ TV);
16: Remove old references between $n_{new}.T_{\succ}$ and $n_{new}.T_{\prec}$;
17: **for** each node n in G, $n.t \succ n_{new}.t$ **do**
18:     $n.c \leftarrow n.c + 1$;
19:     **if** $n.c \geq k - 1$ **then**
20:         Remove all nodes in $n.T_{\succ}$ in cascade style;
21:     **end if**
22: **end for**

---

set of tuples with rank just lower than t, i.e., (i) $\forall t' \in T_{\succ}, t' \succ t$, and (ii) $\nexists t', t'' \in T_{\succ}$ that $t' \succ t''$. The entry *state* records the state of the node, within {TV (To Visit), VD (Visited), NV (No Visit)}. The entry c is the number of tuples in the *domGraph* with rank higher than t.

Algorithm maintainDomGraph (Algorithm 7) shows how to maintain *domGraph* when a new tuple t arrives. Initially, three First In First Out (FIFO) queues, Q, $Q_{\prec}$ and $Q_{\succ}$, which store nodes to be visited, dominating t, and dominated by t respectively are emptied. Recall that pop(Q) and push(n, Q) are basic operators for an FIFO queue. The operator pop(Q) returns the item at the front of a non-empty queue Q, and then removes it from Q. Otherwise, it returns *NULL* if Q is empty. The operator **push**(n, Q) inserts item n at the back of the queue Q. The subroutine **set**$(nodes, st)$ updates the *state* of any node in *nodes* to st. For example, at line 1, **set**(G, TV) means that the states of all nodes in G are set to TV. The variable b, initialized to zero, represents the number of nodes visited.

At first, All nodes in G, but not dominated by any other node, are pushed into Q (lines 1–4). Subsequently, it begins to construct two FIFO queues, $Q_\prec$ and $Q_\succ$, by processing all nodes in Q (lines 5–14). The queue $Q_\prec$ represents all nodes that just dominate t, and $Q_\succ$ represents all nodes that are just dominated by t. The state of the node popped from Q, n, is updated to VD (visited), meaning that node n *has been visited*. Obviously, any node that dominates $n.t$ also dominates t if $n.t \prec t$, so that it is unnecessary to visit these nodes in future. Under such situation, we begin to compare $n.c$ with k. It is clear that the new tuple t will not be a candidate if $n.c \geq k - 1$ so that the processing for t can be terminated. Otherwise, we push n into $Q_\prec$, and set the states of all nodes in $n.T_\prec$ NV (not visit). A node with a state of NV will never be pushed into Q. Subsequently, if $t \prec n.t$, we push n into $Q_\succ$, and update $Q_\succ$ to make it only contain nodes directly dominated by t. Note that we need to check all nodes dominating t if the tuple t is not dominated by $n.t$. In this way, the subroutine **pushDominated** (Algorithm 8) is invoked immediately to push some nodes in $n.T_\prec$ into Q if the following two conditions hold simultaneously (i) with a state of TV, and (ii) all nodes dominated by such nodes have been visited. Condition (i) claims that a node to be pushed into Q has not been visited. Condition (ii) shows that

---

Algorithm 8 pushDominated(n, Q)

1: **for** each node n' in $n.T_\prec$ **do**
2:    **if** n'.state = TV **then**
3:       push(n', Q) if $\forall n'' \in n'.T_\succ$, n''.state = VD;
4:    **end if**
5: **end for**

---

a node is pushed into Q after all nodes dominated by it have been visited.

Then, it inserts a new node for t into G if necessary. The queues $Q_\prec$ and $Q_\succ$ keep all nodes dominating t and dominated by t respectively. We compute the entry c, which represents the number of nodes dominating t in G. Since all nodes dominating any node in $Q_\prec$ have not been visited (labeled as NV), and b represents the number of nodes been visited, there are $|G| + |Q_\prec| - b$ nodes in G dominating t. Subsequently, we remove all references between $n_{new}.T_\succ$ and $n_{new}.T_\prec$ to make G consistent (lines 15–16).

Finally, for each node dominated by t, the entry c increases by 1. If we find a node n such that $n.c \geq k - 1$, all nodes dominated by n can be removed safely (lines 17–21).

Maintaining *domGraph* significantly reduces the space consumption since the tuples that are not candidates can be removed safely. Moreover, *domGaph* is efficient to maintain. Without this directed acyclic graph, it is inconvenient to decide whether the new tuple is a candidate or not. In our algorithm, we compare the new tuple with a set of low-ranked tuples in G at first, so that the decision can be made quickly.

Example 3.6. Figure 3.4 illustrates the evolution of a *domGraph* based on the data in Figure 3.2. Let $k = 2$. Each node is affiliated with tuple t and entry c. A directed link from n_i to n_j means $n_i.t \prec n_j.t$. Obviously, A *domGraph* is a directed acyclic graph. After time 2, both t_1 and t_2 stay in domGraph and $t_1 \succ t_2$. At time 3, since $t_1 \prec t_3$ and $n_1.c = 1 \geq k - 1$, t_3 will not be inserted into *domGraph*. In this way, the next three tuples will be inserted into the *domGraph*.

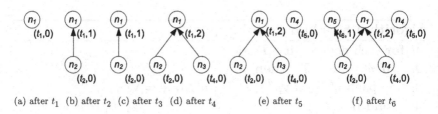

(a) after t_1 (b) after t_2 (c) after t_3 (d) after t_4 (e) after t_5 (f) after t_6

Fig. 3.4   The evolution of domGraph based on Figure 3.2

On-demand query processing. ER-Top$k$ query can be processed efficiently by using *domGraph* and *probTree*. Initially, an FIFO queue Q and a result set R are emptied. Let $r_{max}(R)$ denote the maximal expected rank of all nodes in R, i.e., $r_{max}(R) = \max_{n \in R}(r(n))$. At first, all nodes not dominated by any other node are pushed into Q since these nodes may be at the 1st rank. Subsequently, a node (n) is popped out of Q for evaluation repeatedly until Q is empty. The expected rank $r(n)$ is computed by Equation (3.1). If R has no more than k nodes, node n is added into R immediately. Otherwise, only when $r(n) < r_{max}(R)$, we insert n into R to replace the lowest-ranked tuple. Next, we check whether each node (say, n') in $n.T_{\succ}$ should be pushed into Q or not. In general, n' is inserted into Q under two conditions. First, all nodes dominating n' are in R. Otherwise, if parts of such nodes are still in Q, it is no need pushing n' into R so early; if parts of such nodes have been processed but cannot be kept in R, it means n' cannot belong to the result set. Second, the size of R is not full or $r_{max}(n'.T_{\prec}) < r_{max}(R)$.

3.3 Handling TTk and aTTk Queries

TTk query can be processed by using *probTree*, as described in Algorithm 9. The set R stores all candidate tuples satisfying $r_j(t_j) \leq \tau$. When a new tuple t_i arrives, the algorithm updates *probTree*, computes t_i's ranking score, and inserts t_i into R if $r_i(t_i) \leq \tau$ holds. At any time point, all tuples in R meet the query requirement (lines 4–6). Moreover, if the users are only interested in the tuples with global ranking score below τ, i.e., $r_i(t) \leq \tau$, we continue to execute lines 7–12 periodically. The rank of each tuple in R is recomputed by using the *probTree* T. The space consumption is $O(Z)$, and the per-tuple processing cost is $O(x \cdot \log Z)$.

However, the space complexity of Algorithm 9 is high when there are too many distinct values in the data stream, which makes it necessary to devise a new solution. Besides a *probTree* T, our new solution (Algorithm 10) also uses a novel ES buffer B. The *probTree* T only stores a small part of input data, while the ES buffer B stores some samples. An ES buffer B has L levels, denoted as

---

Algorithm 9 processTTk()

1: Empty a probTree T;
2: Empty a set R that stores all result tuples;
3: **while** a tuple t_i arrives **do**
4: Insert t_i into the *probTreeT*;
5: Compute the expected rank $r_i(t_i)$ based on T;
6: Update $R \leftarrow R \cup \{t_i\}$ if $r_i(t_i) \le \tau$;
   // Lines 7-12 are executed for tuples with global ranking score below τ
7: **if** at the edge of every period **then**
8:   **for** each tuple t in R **do**
9:    Update the rank of t by using T;
10:   Remove t from R if its ranking score $> \tau$;
11: **end for**
12: **end if**
13: **end while**

Algorithm 10 processATTk(ϵ, δ, τ, N, s)

1: $L = \lceil \log_2 \frac{N\epsilon^2 s}{32 \ln(2/\delta)} \rceil$; $\quad H \leftarrow \lceil \frac{4\ln(2L/\delta)}{(\epsilon/2)^2} \rceil$; $\quad sump \leftarrow 0$;
2: Create a new probTree T and an ES buffer B;
3: **while** a new tuple t_i arrives **do**
4: **for** each pair $(v_{i,j}, p_{i,j})$ **do**
5:   Insert $(v_{i,j}, p_{i,j})$ into T if $|B_0| < H$ or $v_{i,j} \ge$ value(B_0, H);
6: **end for**
7: Remove all entries (say, e) in T satisfying $e.v <$ value(B_0, H);
8: handleTuple(t_i, B, s, L, H);
9: Output t_i if estimateER(t_i, T, B, $sump$) $\ge \tau$;
10: Update $sump \leftarrow sump + \sum p_j i, j$;
11: **end while**

$B_0, B_1, \ldots, B_{L-1}$. Each level stores a number of samples generated from the data stream, but with different sampling rate. So far we focus on the main body of Algorithm 10, and leave the details of ES later. Figure 3.5 illustrates the main difference between Algorithm processTTk and Algorithm processATTk.

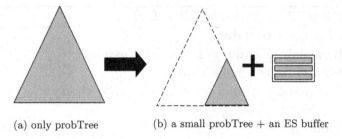

(a) only probTree   (b) a small probTree + an ES buffer

Fig. 3.5   Data structures in TTk vs. aTTk

Algorithm 11 estimateER(t_i, T, B, *sump*)

1: $er \leftarrow 0$;
2: **for** each pair $(v_{i,j}, p_{i,j})$ of t_i **do**
3:      **if** $v_{i,j} > \mathsf{value}(B_0, H)$ **then**
4:          $er \leftarrow er + p_{i,j} \cdot q(v_{i,j})$;   //using T
5:      **else**
6:          $er \leftarrow er + p_{i,j} \cdot \mathsf{getq}(v_{i,j})$;   //using B
7:      **end if**
8:      $er \leftarrow er - p_{i,j} \cdot q_i(v_{i,j})$;
9: **end for**
10: $er \leftarrow er + sump \cdot (1 - \sum_j p_{i,j})$;
11: **return** er;

Algorithm processATTk uses five parameters: ϵ, δ, τ, N, and s, where ϵ, δ, and τ are the query parameters in Definition 3.3, N the stream length and s the sampling parameter of the ES buffer. At first, it sets two key parameters for an ES buffer B: L and H. When a new tuple t_i arrives, each pair (say, $(v_{i,j}, p_{i,j})$) will be inserted into T immediately either when there are no more than H samples in B_0 or $v_{i,j} \geq \mathsf{value}(B_0, H)$. We also check T frequently to remove the entries smaller than $\mathsf{value}(B_0, H)$ (lines 4–7). Subsequently, handleTuple (Algorithm 12) is invoked to maintain B. Then, estimateER (Algorithm 11) is invoked to estimate the expected rank of t_i to decide whether to output t_i or not. Finally, the variable *sump* that represents the sum of the probabilities of all tuples till now is updated (lines 8–10).

Algorithm 12 handleTuple(t, B, s, L, H)

1: **for** $l = L - 1$ **to** 0 **do**
2:      Randomly generate $s/2^l$ samples based on t;
3:      **for** each *valid* sample v **do**
4:          **if** $(l = L - 1)$ **or** $(v \geq \mathsf{value}(B_{l+1}, H))$ **then**
5:              Insert v into B_l;
6:          **end if**
7:      **end for**
8:      **if** $l < L - 1$ **then**
9:          $\Psi \leftarrow \{v' \mid v' \in B_l \wedge v' \leq \mathsf{value}(B_{l+1}, H)\}$;
10:         **if** $|B_l - \Psi| \geq H$ **then**
11:             $B_l \leftarrow B_l - \Psi$;
12:         **end if**
13:     **end if**
14: **end for**

Algorithm estimateER (Algorithm 11) estimates the expected rank of a new tuple. For each item $(v_{i,j}, p_{i,j})$, if $v_{i,j} > \mathsf{value}(B_0, H)$, we get $q(v_{i,j})$ from T exactly. Otherwise, we get $q(v_{i,j})$ from B approximately. Besides, we also need to consider the probability distribution function of each tuple (lines 3–8). Finally, the existential confidence of t_i cannot be ignored (line 10). See Equation (3.1) for details.

Exponential Sampling. An ES buffer B has L levels, denoted as $B_0, B_1, \ldots, B_{L-1}$. Each level stores a number of samples generated from the data stream, but with different sampling rates. The sampling parameter s controls the sampling rate at different levels. The sampling rate of the lth level, B_l, is $s/2^l$. For example, the sampling rates of the first level B_0 and the last level B_{L-1} are s and $s/2^{L-1}$ respectively. For simplicity, we set the value of s to the power of 2, making $s/2^l$ either an integer or a real value in $(0, 1)$. An ES buffer also uses parameter H to restrict the memory consumption.

An ES buffer has two key operators, handleTuple and getq. When a new tuple arrives, handleTuple (Algorithm 12) repeats to generate

$s/2^l$ samples in average for all l levels in B. In other words, if $s/2^l \geq 1$, it generates $s/2^l$ samples in random; otherwise, it only generates one sample with probability $s/2^l$. In addition, each sample only has a confidence smaller than 1 to be *valid* if the new tuple also has existential uncertainty. Let $\mathsf{value}(B_l, H)$ denote a subroutine that returns a sample in B_l ranked at the Hth place. Especially, this subroutine returns a virtual minimum value if the number of samples in B_l is smaller than H, i.e., $|B_l| < H$.

For the levels (say, l) other than the last level, i.e., $l < L - 1$, the samples (say, v) satisfying $v \geq \mathsf{value}(B_{l+1}, H)$ are inserted into B_l immediately. Otherwise, the samples are discarded at once. For the last level B_{L-1}, the valid samples are inserted into this level immediately (lines 3–7). The next task is to remove parts of samples to save the memory space with the following two policies: (i) the samples in the last level B_{L-1} will not be removed at all; (ii) the samples in the rest levels (say, B_l, $l < L - 1$) are dropped if they are smaller than $\mathsf{value}(B_{l+1}, H)$. Note that the size of each level must be above H after removing parts of samples (lines 8–13).

The operator getq (Algorithm 13) can estimate the value of $q(v)$. Given any v, it looks for the first level B_l that satisfies $v \geq \mathsf{value}(B_{l+1}, H)$, and returns $\mathsf{rank}(B_l, v) \cdot 2^l/s$. Note that the subroutine $\mathsf{rank}(B_l, v)$ returns the number of samples greater than v in B_l. If there exists no such l, it estimates $q(v)$ from B_0.

Algorithm 13 $\mathsf{getq}(v,\ B)$

1: **if** $|B_0| < H$ **or** $v > \mathsf{value}(B_0, H)$ **then**
2:    **return** $\mathsf{rank}(B_0, v)/s$;
3: **end if**
4: $l \leftarrow L - 1$;
5: **for** $i = 0$ **to** $L - 2$ **do**
6:    **if** $\mathsf{value}(B_{i+1}, H) \leq v < \mathsf{value}(B_i, H)$ **then**
7:       $l \leftarrow i$; **break**;
8:    **end if**
9: **end for**
10: **return** $\mathsf{rank}(B_l, v) \cdot 2^l/s$;

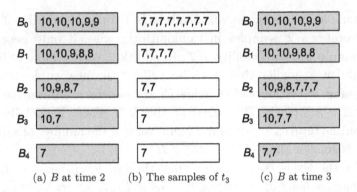

(a) B at time 2   (b) The samples of t_3 (c) B at time 3

Fig. 3.6 An example of exponential sampling

Example 3.7. Consider the small dataset in Figure 3.2. We create an ES buffer B by setting: $L = 5$, $s = 8$ and $H = 4$. Assuming the state of B at time 2 and the samples of t_3 are listed in Figures 3.6(a) and 3.6(b) respectively in one run, we show how to maintain B at time 3. At first, $\{70\}$ is inserted into B_4 and B_3 respectively. Second, $\{7, 7\}$ is inserted into B_2. The other buffers are unaffected since all existing samples are greater than 7.

The value of $q(v)$ can be estimated by using B conveniently. The key step is to find the appropriate level. For example, since $\mathsf{rank}(B_2, 7) = 4$ and $\mathsf{value}(B_2, H) > 7 \geq \mathsf{value}(B_1, H)$, $q(v)$ is estimated as $4 \times 2^2/8 = 2$. Similarly, we use B_1 to estimate $q(8)$: $\mathsf{getq}(8, B) = 4 \times 2^1/8 = 1$. These values are close to the exact values: $q(7) = 1.3$, and $q(8) = 0.7$.

We show for any v, $v < \mathsf{value}(B_0, H)$, there exists a level B_l such that (i) $v < \mathsf{value}(B_l, H)$ and (ii) $v \geq \mathsf{value}(B_{l+1}, H)$ if B_{l+1} exists. Hence, let ϵ denote the error parameter, δ the probability parameter and s the sampling parameter, $0 < \epsilon, \delta < 1$. Let $H = \lceil \frac{4\ln(2/\delta)}{\epsilon^2} \rceil$. $\forall v$, if $q(v) \geq \frac{4\ln(2/\delta)}{s\epsilon^2}$, the result computed by the getq operator satisfies the ϵ–δ constraint. In other words, the relative error of the estimated value is smaller than ϵ with probability at least $1 - \delta$ [52].

An ES buffer is also capable of estimating a $q(\cdot)$ expression E that is the sum of several $q(\cdot)$ functions, i.e., $E = \sum_{i=1}^{c} a_i q(v_i)$, where

---

Algorithm 14 getqExp(E, B)

1: Assume E is described as $E = \sum_{i=1}^{c} a_i q(v_i)$;
2: *result* $\leftarrow$ 0;
3: **for** $i = 1$ **to** c **do**
4:    *result* $\leftarrow$ *result* $+ a_i \cdot$ getq(v_i);
5: **end for**
6: **return** *result*;

Algorithm 15 value(T, H)

1: *sum* $\leftarrow$ 0; $e \leftarrow T.root$;   *result* $\leftarrow$ MIN_VALUE;
2: **while** $e \neq NULL$ **do**
3:   **if** *sum* $+ e.p > H$ **then**
4:     *result* $\leftarrow e.v$; $e \leftarrow e.r$;
5:   **else**
6:     *sum* $\leftarrow$ *sum* $+ e.p$; $e \leftarrow e.l$;
7:   **end if**
8: **end while**
9: **return** *result*;

$\forall 1 \leq i \leq c$, $a_i > 0$. The operator getqExp (Algorithm 14) estimates an expression.

Theorem 3.1. Consider a $q(\cdot)$ expression $E = \sum_{j=1}^{c} a_j \cdot q(v_j)$, where $a_j > 0$ holds for any j. Let ϵ denote the error parameter, and δ the probability parameter, $0 < \epsilon, \delta < 1$. Let $H = \lceil \frac{4\ln(2L/\delta)}{\epsilon^2} \rceil$. If $q(\max_{1 \leq j \leq c}(v_j)) \geq H/s$, the estimate satisfies the ϵ–δ constraint.

Another issue is how to implement an ES buffer efficiently. Algorithm handleTuple (Algorithm 12) that invokes value(B_l, H) several times is also invoked frequently. The performance will be reduced if all samples are stored out of order. Here, we use a *probTree* instead: we insert a pair $(v, 1)$ into the tree when a new sample v comes. Now, executing value(B_l, H) costs $O(\log |T|)$, where $|T|$ is the number of entries in T (Algorithm 15). Moreover, compression is another benefit to use *probTree*. For example, in Figure 3.6(c), there

---

Algorithm 16 rank(T, v)

1: $sum \leftarrow 0$;　　$e \leftarrow T.root$;
2: **while** $e \neq NULL$ **do**
3:　　**if** $e.v > v$ **then**
4:　　　　$sum \leftarrow sum + e.p$;　　$e \leftarrow e.l$;
5:　　**else**
6:　　　　$e \leftarrow e.r$;
7:　　**end if**
8: **end while**
9: **return** sum;

---

are three identical samples in the first level B_0. By using *probTree*, all identical samples are aggregated at one entry.

Algorithm 13 estimates $q(v)$. It also uses rank(B_l, v) (Algorithm 16) in the last line. By using the *probTree*, the executing cost is $O(\log |T|)$, where $|T|$ is the number of entries in T.

Performance analysis. The expected rank of each tuple estimated by estimateER satisfies ϵ-δ constraint [52]. We analyze the performance of the proposed solution. Our solution uses two main structures: a *probTree T* and an ES buffer B. At Line 7 of processATTk, all entries (say, e) with $e.v <$ value(B_0, H) are removed from T to save space. The sum of the probabilities of all entries in T is around H/s. The size of T is sensitive to the average probability of input entries. If each entry tends to have small probability, we need to maintain more entries in T.

Contrarily, the ES buffer B is insensitive to the average probability of each entry. Any of the first $L - 1$ levels costs $O(H)$ space, and the last level (B_{L-1}) costs $O(Ns/2^{L-1})$ since the sampling rate is $s/2^{L-1}$. Hence, the total space consumption of B is $O(LH + Ns/2^{L-1})$. When L decreases, the last level needs more space.

If the stream length N is given in advance, we can set L to make each level have similar size. We have: $Ns/2^{L-1} \approx 2H$. Equally, $\frac{Ns}{2^{L-1}} \approx 2\lceil \frac{4\ln(2L/\delta)}{(\epsilon/2)^2} \rceil$. In general, $1 < L < 2/\delta$. Thus, $\ln(2/\delta) < \ln(2L/\delta) < 2\ln(2/\delta)$. Hence, we simply set the value of

L to $\lceil \log_2 \frac{Ns\epsilon^2}{32\ln(2/\delta)} \rceil$.[1] Under this condition, the space consumption of B is $O(\ln(Ns\epsilon^2)\epsilon^{-2}\ln(\delta^{-1}))$.

Note that s balances the space consumption of T and B. When s increases, the size of T decreases, whereas the size of B increases.

3.4 Experimental Results

In this section, we present an experimental study upon synthetic and real data. The source code was written in C++. The experiments to test ER-Top$k$ query were performed on a system with Intel Core 2 CPU (2.4GHz) and 4G memory, while that to test threshold-based ER-Top$k$ query were conducted on a system with Intel Core i5-2410 CPU and 3G memory.

Dataset description. We use five datasets. The first three are synthetic, while the last two are generated from a real dataset.

- **syn-uni**. This set contains 20,000,000 tuples. It only has *existential* uncertainty. The rank of each tuple is randomly selected from 1 to 20 million without replacement and the probability is uniformly distributed in $(0, 1)$.
- **syn-nor**. This set contains 20,000,000 tuples. It has both kinds of uncertainties. The existential confidence of each tuple, denoted as p_i, is randomly generated from a normal distribution $N(0.6, 0.3)$.[2] We set the maximal number of options of all tuples no more than 10, i.e., $s_{\max} = 10$. For the ith tuple, the number of the attribute options (say, s_i) is uniformly selected from $[s_{\max}/2, s_{\max}]$. Subsequently, we construct a normal distribution $N(\mu_i, \sigma_i)$, where μ_i is uniformly selected from $[0, 1000]$ and σ_i is uniformly selected from $[0, 1]$. We randomly select s_i values from $N(\mu_i, \sigma_i)$, denoted as $v_1, \ldots, v_{s_i}$, and construct this tuple as $\langle (v_1, p_i/s_i), \ldots, (v_i, p_i/s_i) \rangle$.

---

[1] If the value of L turns to be greater than $2/\delta$, we use the inequality $\ln(2L/\delta) < 3\ln(2/\delta)$ instead, and so forth. In this way, we can decide the value of L conveniently.

[2] $N(\mu, \sigma)$ is a normal distribution with μ as mean value and σ as standard deviation.

- **Nor-$s_{\max}$.** This set contains 1,000,000 tuples. For each tuple t_i, we first generate a normal distribution $N(\mu_i, \sigma_i^2)$ where the mean μ_i and the standard deviation σ_i are uniformly selected from the ranges $[1, 10^7]$ and $[10^3, 10^4]$ respectively. Let $s_{\max}$ denote the maximal number of options per tuple, and s_i denote the number of items that is uniformly selected from $[1, s_{\max}]$. Thus, t_i is represented as $\langle (v_{i,1}, \frac{1}{s_i}), \ldots, (v_{i,s_i}, \frac{1}{s_i}) \rangle$ after s_i samples (say, $v_{i,1}, \ldots, v_{i,s_i}$) being selected from $N(\mu_i, \sigma_i^2)$.

- **UncertainIIP.** This dataset is also used in Chapter 2. See Section 2.5 for details.

- **IIP-$s_{\max}$.** We construct this dataset by repeatedly selecting 1,000,000 records from the IIP dataset that is introduced in Section 2.5. The number of days drifted, μ_i, is treated as the ranking score. Given an integer $s_{\max}$, each tuple is formatted as $\langle (v_{i,1}, \frac{1}{s_{\max}}), \ldots, (v_{i,s_i}, \frac{1}{s_{\max}}) \rangle$ after selecting s_i samples (say, $v_{i,1}, \ldots, v_{i,s_i}$) uniformly from a range of $[0.9\mu_i, 1.1\mu_i]$, where the values of s_i for seven different confidence levels are $\lceil s_{\max} \rceil$, $\lceil \frac{9}{10} s_{\max} \rceil$, $\lceil \frac{8}{10} s_{\max} \rceil$, $\lceil \frac{7}{10} s_{\max} \rceil$, $\lceil \frac{6}{10} s_{\max} \rceil$, $\lceil \frac{5}{10} s_{\max} \rceil$ or $\lceil \frac{6}{10} s_{\max} \rceil$ respectively.

Testing ER-Top$k$ query. We first evaluate the space-complexity. Our solution can prune parts of tuples efficiently, while the static method must keep all information in memory. The space-complexity is quite high when such information is huge.

Figure 3.7 illustrates that the space consumption of the proposed method. In general, each tuple also contains information other than the scoring attributes. For example, the IIP dataset contains 19 attributes, including 2 time fields, 7 category fields and 10 numeric fields, among which only two fields are used for the scoring function and confidence respectively. All such information must be stored if a tuple may belong to the query result. The x-axis in Figures 3.7(a) and 3.7(b), representing the size of such information per tuple, varies from 10 to 1,000. The *domGraph* size is small, since only a small number of tuples are stored. The *probTree* size is decided by the number of distinct attribute values, independent of the information attributes. Figure 3.7(c) illustrates the space consumption upon the

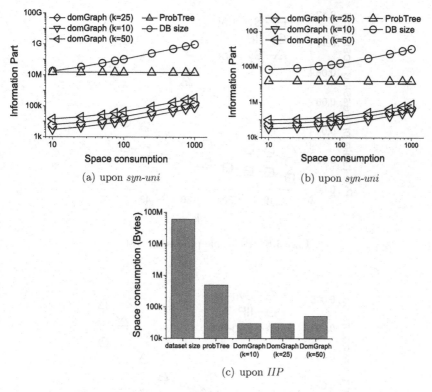

(a) upon *syn-uni*

(b) upon *syn-uni*

(c) upon *IIP*

Fig. 3.7 Space consumption upon uncertain datasets

IIP dataset, where each tuple uses 52 bytes to store the information attributes. The space consumption is only 1% of the total dataset.

Figure 3.8 illustrates that the per-tuple processing cost is low on three uncertain datasets. When k increases, the cost continues to grow. The cost for *syn-nor* is significantly higher than that for the other datasets, since each tuple in *syn-nor* contains multiple attribute choices, which increases the cost on maintaining *probTree*.

Figure 3.9 illustrates the cost on handling a request upon three datasets with the comparison of the static method. The x-axis represents parameter k, and the y-axis represents time cost. Similarly, when k increases, the cost continues to grow. The cost on *syn-nor* and IIP is significantly greater than that on *syn-uni* due to two reasons. First, the *syn-nor* dataset has multiple choices in the scoring

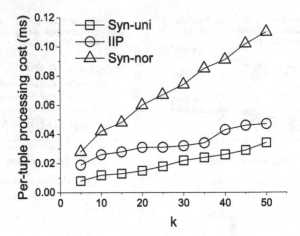

Fig. 3.8   Per-tuple processing cost

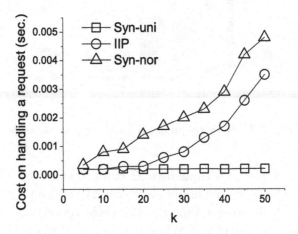

Fig. 3.9   Cost on handling a request

attribute, making it expensive to compute the rank of each candidate tuple. Second, the *domGraph* for IIP is more complex than that for *syn-uni* due to many identical tuples. Anyway, this cost can be reduced significantly if we can scan the *domGraph* conveniently with the help of an additional list for candidates.

Testing threshold-based ER-Top$k$. Figure 3.10 reports the per-tuple processing cost and the space consumption upon the data

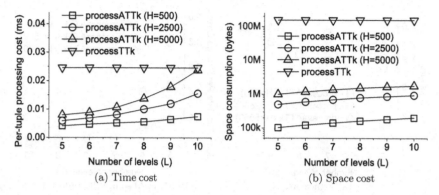

Fig. 3.10 Efficiency tests upon the data stream *Nor*-30

stream *Nor*-30. The x-axis represents the number of levels of B. The threshold parameter τ is set to 500 for two approaches. The sum of the probabilities of all items in T is limited to 10. Under all situations, processATTk runs faster than processTTk due to two reasons. First, although each method maintains a *probTree* in memory, the size of the tree in processTTk is much more complex than that in processATTk since the former stores all distinct elements in the data stream while the latter only stores a few. Second, when t_i arrives, processTTk needs to update the *probTree* for s_i times. Contrarily, the maintenance cost of B is nearly independent of s_i. The performance gap between two approaches becomes narrower when L or H grows. The per-tuple processing cost of processATTk is strongly related to the size of B. When B has more levels (i.e., L rises), or stores more samples per level (i.e., H rises), the per-tuple processing cost will increase accordingly.

Figure 3.10(b) shows that processATTk is space-efficient. Assuming each entry in a *probTree* uses 20 bytes (including 3 pointers and 2 float numbers), processATTk consumes no more than 2MB in all situations, while processTTk consumes more than 150MB. In addition, the space consumption of processATTk is nearly linear to H or L.

Figure 3.11 reports the effectiveness, including F-measure and Mean Absolute Percentage Error (MAPE). F-measure is the harmonic mean of precision and recall. Let A denote a set of target

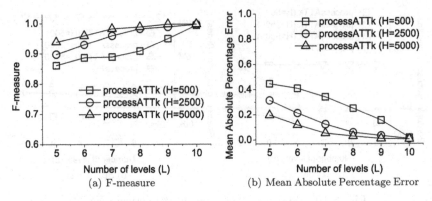

(a) F-measure   (b) Mean Absolute Percentage Error

Fig. 3.11   Effectiveness tests upon the data stream Nor-30

elements, and $\hat{A}$ a set of elements obtained by some algorithm. F-measure $= \frac{2 \times \text{precision} \times \text{recall}}{\text{precision}+\text{recall}}$ where precision $= |A \cap \hat{A}|/|\hat{A}|$, and recall $= |A \cap \hat{A}|/|A|$. Figure 3.11(a) illustrates the change of F-measure under different conditions. When L or H rises, F-measure approaches to 1. Specially, when $L = 10$, the F-measure value is above 0.99.

Mean Absolute Percentage Error (MAPE) is popular to measure the quality of the query results. Remember that $r_i(t_i)$ denotes the expected rank of t_i. Let $\hat{r}_i(t_i)$ denote the estimator obtained by estimateER, and R the set containing all tuples with estimated expected rank no greater than τ, i.e., $R = \{t_i | \hat{r}_i(t_i) \leq \tau\}$. MAPE $= \left(\sum_{t_i \in R} |r_i(t_i) - \hat{r}_i(t_i)| \right)/|R|$. Figure 3.11(b) illustrates the change of MAPE under different conditions. When L or H increases, MAPE continues to decrease. Specially, when $L = 10$, MAPE is below 2%; when $L = 9 \wedge H \geq 2500$, MAPE is below 4%.

Figure 3.12 reports the executing cost upon different data streams. Let $\tau = 500$, $L = 9$ and $H = 2500$. The x-axis represents the $s_{\max}$ parameter. The greater $s_{\max}$ means more items per tuple in the stream. Under all situations, processATTk runs faster and consumes less space than processTTk. When $s_{\max}$ increases, the gap between two approaches becomes much more significant. When $s_{\max}$ changes, the space consumption of processATTk almost remains unchanged, since the ES buffer B is independent of the tuple's

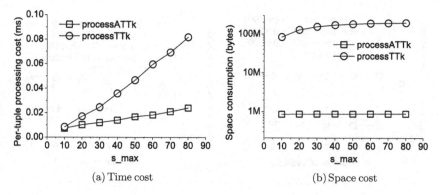

(a) Time cost   (b) Space cost

Fig. 3.12 Performance evaluation upon the data stream $Nor\text{-}s_{\max}$

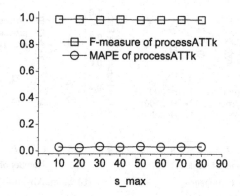

Fig. 3.13 Effectiveness tests upon $Nor\text{-}s_{\max}$

complexity. Contrarily, the increment of $s_{\max}$ may result in higher space consumption since the size of the *probTree* T is dependent of the number of distinct items in the data stream. We observe the space consumption of processTTk increases from 84MB to 195MB when $s_{\max}$ varies from 10 to 80. Note that a data stream $Nor\text{-}s_{\max}$ contains at most 10M distinct items in the data stream, so that processTTk consumes at most 200MB space.

Figure 3.13 reports the effectiveness of processATTk upon different data streams. Both measures almost remain unchanged when $s_{\max}$ increases from 10 to 80.

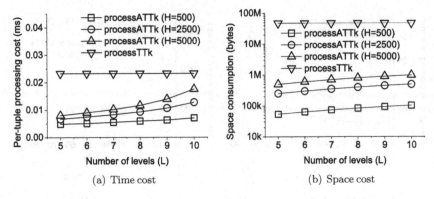

(a) Time cost

(b) Space cost

Fig. 3.14   Efficiency tests upon the data stream *IIP*-20

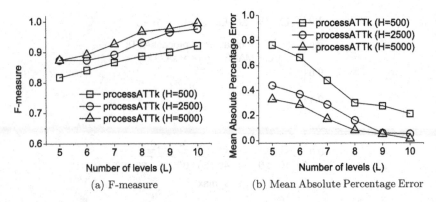

(a) F-measure

(b) Mean Absolute Percentage Error

Fig. 3.15   Effectiveness tests upon the data stream *IIP*-20

Figures 3.14 and 3.15 report the performance upon the *IIP*-20 data stream. The trend is similar to that on the synthetic data streams. When the number of levels (L) or the number of samples per level (H) grows, both per-tuple processing cost and space consumption of the approximate solution rise. However, compared with the exact solution, the resource consumption is still economical. For example, even when $L = 10$ and $H = 5,000$, the per-tuple processing cost is 30% cheaper than that of the exact solution. The approximate solution is significantly more space-efficient than the exact one. Under all situations, the approximate solution only uses no more than 1M bytes, while the exact solution needs more than 40M bytes. Figure 3.15 compares F-measure and MAPE under different parameter settings. Obviously, when L or H increases, both metrics behave better. Especially, when $L = 10$ and $H = 5,000$, F-measure is above 0.99 and MAPE is only around 0.012.

Chapter 4

Rarity Estimation

4.1 Problem Definition

The α-rarity for deterministic data is the proportion of distinct elements with frequency equal to α. A simple extension to uncertain data is to view the sum of the probabilities of all tuples for each element as the frequency of that element. For example, Table 4.1 illustrates a small data stream of iceberg observations in 2005 from the International Ice Patrol (IIP).[1] Each record contains information about the sighting date and time, location, and the way of sighting, such as R/V (Radar and visual, converted to 0.8 confidence) and VIS (visual only, converted to 0.7 confidence). There are three icebergs (e.g., 1, 2, 3), and their frequencies are 1.5($= 0.8 + 0.7$), 0.8, and 0.8 respectively. According to traditional definition, when $\alpha = 1.5$, the rarity is equal to $1/3$; when $\alpha = 0.8$, the rarity is equal to $2/3$; otherwise, rarity is zero. However, under this semantics, the domain of α changes to real numbers, no longer integers. Moreover, this traditional model does not support possible world semantics. Hence, we need to extend the semantics to uncertain data by overcoming these weaknesses.

Table 4.2 illustrates in total 12 possible worlds for the data stream in Table 4.1. The rarity in each possible world is computed directly since a possible world is actually a deterministic dataset.

---

[1]http://nsidc.org/data/g00807.html.

Table 4.1   A Small Data Stream of Iceberg Observations

Record ID	Iceberg ID	Sighting Date and Time	Latitude/ Longitude	Confidence	Probability
1	1	02/23/2005 12:00	48.41/−51.50	R/V	0.8
2	2	02/23/2005 12:00	48.76/−52.98	R/V	0.8
3	3	02/23/2005 12:00	48.71/−52.93	R/V	0.8
4	1	03/01/2005 16:56	48.53/−50.58	VIS	0.7

For example, both 1-rarity and 2-rarity in pw_6 are 0.5. We extend the semantics by using the expected rarity upon all possible worlds. In this case, the expected 1-rarity and 2-rarity are 0.767 and 0.23 respectively.

Let S denote an uncertain data stream containing N tuples, $S = \{t_1, t_2, \ldots, t_N\}$, and each tuple t_i has p_i confidence to exist. Without loss of generality, we assume there are at most m distinct elements, and each tuple is an integer in $[1, m]$. We define α-*uncertain rarity* and *top rarity* below.

Definition 4.1 (α-Uncertain Rarity, ρ_α). Let PW denote the possible world space for an uncertain data stream S. The α-uncertain rarity, ρ_α, is defined as:

$$\rho_\alpha(S) = \sum_{pw \in PW} \left(\frac{\mathsf{rare}(pw, \alpha)}{\mathsf{distinct}(pw)} \cdot \mathbf{Pr}\,[pw] \right), \qquad (4.1)$$

where $\mathsf{distinct}(pw)$ returns the number of distinct elements in pw, and $\mathsf{rare}(pw, \alpha)$ returns the number of elements in pw occurring exactly α times.

Definition 4.2 (Top Rarity). Let PW denote the possible world space for an uncertain data stream S. The top-rarity of S, ξ, is defined as:

$$\xi(S) = argmax_\alpha(\rho_\alpha(S)). \qquad (4.2)$$

Example 4.1. Consider the data stream in Table 4.1. We have: $\rho_1 = 0.767$, $\rho_2 = 0.23$, and $\xi = 1$.

Table 4.2 The Possible Worlds of Example 4.1

ID	Possible world	Probability	1-rarity	2-rarity
pw_1	{1}	0.0152	1.0	0
pw_2	{1,1}	0.0224	0	1.0
pw_3	{3}	0.0096	1.0	0
pw_4	{2}	0.0096	1.0	0
pw_5	{1,3}	0.0608	1.0	0
pw_6	{1,1,3}	0.0896	0.5	0.5
pw_7	{1,2}	0.0608	1.0	0
pw_8	{1,1,2}	0.0896	0.5	0.5
pw_9	{2,3}	0.0384	1.0	0
pw_{10}	{1,2,3}	0.2432	1.0	0
pw_{11}	{1,1,2,3}	0.3584	0.67	0.33
pw_{12}	∅	0.0024	—	—

Expected 1-rarity: 0.767, Expected 2-rarity: 0.23

4.2 An Exact Solution

We begin with an exact method that contains three phases. In *phase 1*, we construct a 2D array A, where each entry, $A[i][j]$, represents the probability that the element i occurs j times in an arbitrary possible world. In *phase 2*, we construct a 2D array B based on A, where each entry, $B[i][j]$, represents the probability that exactly i elements occur exactly j times in an arbitrary possible world. The sizes of A and B are $m \times (g + 1)$ and $(m + 1) \times (m + 1)$ respectively, where m represents the number of distinct elements, and g is the maximal number of identical elements in the dataset. Finally, given a parameter α, we compute ρ_α based on B in the last phase.

Phase 1: constructing 2D array A. A is constructed by scanning S once. Initially, all entries of A are set to zero. When the ith tuple (a_i, p_i) comes, all the entries, $A[a_i][\cdot]$, are affected as follows:

$$A[a_i][j] = \begin{cases} A[a_i][j] \cdot (1 - p_i), & j = 0. \\ A[a_i][j] \cdot (1 - p_i) + A[a_i][j - 1] \cdot p_i, & 1 \le j \le g. \end{cases} \quad (4.3)$$

Since updating an entry $A[a_i][j]$ relies on the old values of $A[a_i][j]$ and $A[a_i][j - 1]$, we update $A[a_i][j]$, $0 \le j \le g$, either in descending order, or using a variable to save the value of $A[a_i][j]$ temporarily if ascending.

Moreover, since the frequency of each element differs a lot, it is unnecessary to allocate $g + 1$ counters for every element. For example, if the element a_i only occurs once in D, it is only necessary to maintain two counters for this element: $A[a_i][0]$ and $A[a_i][1]$. Consequently, we construct a hash table H to represent A. The attribute value a_i is the key in H, and its probability entries, $A[a_i][\cdot]$, are stored in a list.

Algorithm 17 uses a hash table H to process phase 1. The subroutine get(k, H) returns an entry in H with k as the key, or NULL if no such an entry is found. If a_i has not been registered in H yet, a list that has two entries is inserted into H (lines 4–6). Otherwise, we update all entries in L by Equation (4.3). Notice that there is no need to insert a new entry into L if there are already $\alpha + 1$

Algorithm 17 phase1(α)

1: Empty a hash table H;
2: **for** each tuple (a_i, p_i) **do**
3:    $L \leftarrow \mathsf{get}(a_i, H)$;
4:    **if** L is NULL **then**
5:       Insert a new list L_{new} into H with key a_i;
6:       Append two entries, $1 - p_i$ and p_i, into L_{new};
7:    **else**
8:       $x \leftarrow \mathsf{head}(L)$; $c \leftarrow 0$; $v_o = 0$;
9:       **while** $(x \neq NULL)$ **and** $c \leq \alpha$ **do**
10:         $tmp \leftarrow x$;
11:         $x \leftarrow x \cdot (1 - p_i) + v_o \cdot p_i$;
12:         $v_o = tmp$;
13:         $x \leftarrow \mathsf{next}(x, L)$; $c \leftarrow c + 1$;
14:       **end while**
15:       **if** $c \leq \alpha$ **then**
16:         Append a new entry, $v_o \cdot p_i$, into L;
17:       **end if**
18:    **end if**
19: **end for**

---

entries in L. Here, the subroutine $\mathsf{head}(L)$ returns the head element in L, and $\mathsf{next}(t, L)$ refers to the next entry of t in L (lines 8–17). Clearly, it consumes less memory space than A.

Phase 2: constructing array B. It is infeasible to compute the rarity for each possible world since the number of possible worlds is huge. Fortunately, since the rarity values of some possible worlds are identical, we can divide all the possible worlds into a small number of groups to improve efficiency.

We maintain a 2D array $B[\cdot][\cdot]$ with the size of $(m + 1) \cdot (m + 1)$, where m is the number of distinct elements in the data stream. Each entry $B[i][j]$ denotes the sum of the probabilities of all possible worlds where exactly i elements, out of j distinct elements, occur α times. Clearly, α-rarity in all such possible worlds is equal to i/j.

Array B can be maintained by using dynamic programming. Initially, all entries in B are set to zero except $B[0][0] = 1$. Subsequently, for each element l, the array B is updated by Equation (4.4).

$$B[i][j] = \begin{cases} B[i][j] \cdot A[l][0], & i = 0 \land j = 0, \\ 0, & i > 0 \land j = 0, \\ \begin{aligned} &B[i][j] \cdot A[l][0] \\ &+ B[i][j-1] \cdot (1 - A[l][0] - A[l][\alpha]), \end{aligned} & i = 0 \land j > 0, \\ \begin{aligned} &B[i][j] \cdot A[l][0] + B[i-1][j-1] \cdot A[l][\alpha] \\ &+ B[i][j-1] \cdot (1 - A[l][0] - A[l][\alpha]), \end{aligned} & i > 0 \land j > 0. \end{cases}$$

$$(4.4)$$

The array B is maintained under four conditions. First, if $i = 0 \land j = 0$, no tuple occurs in the possible world, so the probability is computed as $B[i][j] \cdot A[l][0]$. Second, the case $i > 0 \land j = 0$ will not happen at all so that $B[i][j] = 0$. Third, $i = 0 \land j > 0$ describes all the possible worlds containing j distinct elements without any tuple occurring α times. Here, $1 - A[l][0] - A[l][\alpha]$ represents the probability that the element l occurs, but not α times. Finally, we consider the condition $i > 0 \land j > 0$. The item $B[i-1][j-1] \cdot A[l][\alpha]$ represents the sum of the probabilities of all possible worlds (i) containing $j-1$ distinct elements out of the first $l-1$ elements with $i-1$ of them occurring exactly α times, and (ii) the element l occurs α times.

Algorithm 18 illustrates how to maintain the array B based on a hash table H. For each L in the hash table H, the first task is to compute three variables, P_1, P_2 and P_3, representing the probabilities that the element does not occur, occurs α times, and occurs but not α times respectively. Subsequently, all entries in B are updated according to Equation (4.4).

Phase 3: computing rarity. Equation (4.5) computes uncertain rarity.

$$\rho_\alpha(S) = \sum_{i=1}^{m} \sum_{j=1}^{m} \left((i/j) \cdot B[i][j] \right). \tag{4.5}$$

Algorithm 18 phase2(H)

1: Initialize all entries in $B[\cdot][\cdot]$ to zero; $B[0][0] = 1$;

2: **for** each L in H **do**

3:    Scanning L to compute P_1, P_2 and P_3, representing the probability of not occurring, occurring α times, and occurring but not α times respectively.

4:    **for** $j = m$ to 0 **do**

5:      **for** $i = m$ to 0 **do**

6:        Update $B[i][j]$ with P_1, P_2 and P_3 by Equation 4.4;

7:      **end for**

8:    **end for**

9: **end for**

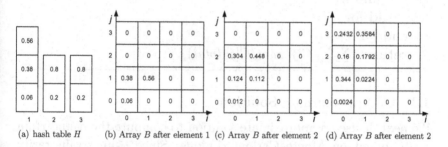

(a) hash table H (b) Array B after element 1   (c) Array B after element 2   (d) Array B after element 2

Fig. 4.1 The middle results of Algorithm 17 and 18 where $\alpha = 2$

For example, Figure 4.1 illustrates the state changes of Table 4.1. $\alpha = 2$. Figure 4.1(a) describes hash table H (an implementation of array A) after executing Algorithm 17. There are three lists in hash table H. Figures 4.1(b)–4.1(d) describe the evolution of B after processing three elements one by one. The sum of the probabilities of array B is equal to 1. The sum of the probabilities at each column remains unchanged, i.e., $\forall i, \sum_{l=0}^{m} B[i][l]$ remains unchanged at any time point.

The time- and space-complexities are $O(m^3)$ and $O(m^2)$ respectively, where m is the number of distinct elements in the data stream.

Algorithm 19 Approximate solution($\alpha, \varepsilon, \delta$)

1: Invoke Algorithm 17 to compute array A;
2: $N = \lceil \ln(2/\delta)\varepsilon^{-2}/2 \rceil$;
3: Empty a new array C with N entries. The jth entry, $C[j]$, is organized as $(part, total)$;
4: **for** $i = 1$ to m **do**
5:   **for** $j = 1$ to N **do**
6:     Flip a coin to generate a random p in $(0, 1)$;
7:     **if** $p \leq A[i][\alpha]$ **then**
8:       $C[j].part \leftarrow C[j].part + 1$;
9:       $C[j].total \leftarrow C[j].total + 1$;
10:      **else if** $p \leq 1 - A[i][0]$ **then**
11:        $C[j].total \leftarrow C[j].total + 1$;
12:     **end if**
13:   **end for**
14: **end for**
15: **return** $\left(\sum_{j=1}^{N} C[j].part/C[j].total \right)/N$;

4.3 An Approximate Solution

We next devise an approximate solution to compute the α-uncertain rarity based on Monte–Carlo technique. Since α-uncertain rarity refers to the expected α-rarity value in all possible worlds (Definition 4.1), it is nature to generate a result by computing the average of all α-rarity values from a number of randomly selected possible world instances, as illustrated in Algorithm 19. First, we invoke Algorithm 17 to generate array A. We also use an array, C, to refer to each possible world. Field $C[j].part$ records the number of items occurring α times in the jth possible world instance, and $C[j].total$ describes the total number of distinct elements in the same possible world. It is convenient to estimate α-uncertain rarity based on array C (lines 3–14). For each element i, we repeat to generate a random value p uniformly in $(0, 1)$ N times. If $p \leq A[i][\alpha]$, it means the element i is selected in this possible world for α times; if $p \leq 1 - A[i][\alpha] - A[i][0]$, it means the element i is selected in this possible world, but not α times. Otherwise, this element does not appear. According to Hoeffding inequality, the result satisfies ε–δ constraint.

The space consumption is $O(N + \ln(2/\delta)\varepsilon^{-2})$, since the size of A is $O(N)$, and the size of C is $O(\ln(2/\delta)\varepsilon^{-2})$. The time complexity is $O(gN + m\ln(2/\delta)\varepsilon^{-2})$, since it costs $O(g \cdot N)$ to generate A, and it costs $O(m\ln(2/\delta)\varepsilon^{-2})$ to maintain C.

4.4 Computing Top Rarity

Next comes how to find a frequency with the maximal rarity, i.e., the top rarity. In a naive method, we compute ρ_α for all $1 \leq \alpha \leq g$ to get the maximal one, where g is the maximal frequency of all elements. However, this method is expensive when g is large because the time complexity is $O(gm^3)$. Fortunately, we find that parts of frequencies can be pruned quickly without computing the rarity values. Let PW denote the possible world space for an uncertain data stream S, and m the number of distinct elements in S, i.e., $m = \max_{pw \in PW}(\mathsf{distinct}(pw))$, $P_\alpha = \sum_{l=1}^{m} A[l][\alpha]$, $\mu = \sum_{l=1}^{m}(1 - A[l][0])$, ε an error parameter, $0 \leq \varepsilon < 1$. Then,

$$P_\alpha/m \leq \rho_\alpha \leq \varepsilon + \frac{P_\alpha}{(1 - \sqrt{2(\ln 1/\varepsilon)/\mu})^2\mu}. \qquad (4.6)$$

We show the proof briefly. Let W denote a random variable of the possible world instance of uncertain dataset U. $\mathsf{rare}(W, \alpha)$ returns the number of elements occurring α times in W, and $\mathsf{distinct}(W)$ returns the distinct number of elements in W. So, we have

$$\mathbf{E}\left[\mathsf{rare}(W, \alpha)\right] = P_\alpha, \qquad (4.7)$$

$$\mathbf{E}\left[\mathsf{distinct}(W)\right] = \mu. \qquad (4.8)$$

According to Definition 4.1, the α-uncertain rarity, ρ_α, is computed below since the expression $\mathsf{distinct}(W) \leq m$ holds for any W.

$$\rho_\alpha(D) = \mathbf{E}\left[\frac{\mathsf{rare}(W, \alpha)}{\mathsf{distinct}(W)}\right] \geq \mathbf{E}\left[\mathsf{rare}(W, \alpha)\right]/m = P_\alpha/m. \qquad (4.9)$$

Moreover, $\forall W$, rare$(W, \alpha) \leq$ distinct(W). Let $\varepsilon \in (0, 1)$. Let $\delta = \sqrt{\frac{2 \ln 1/\varepsilon}{\mu}}$. According to Chernoff bound [12], we have

$$\mathbf{Pr}\left[\text{distinct}(W) < (1 - \delta)\mu\right] < \varepsilon. \tag{4.10}$$

Thus, the upper bound of ρ_α is decided by the following Equation.

$$
\begin{aligned}
\rho_\alpha &= \mathbf{E}\left[\frac{\text{rare}(W, \alpha)}{\text{distinct}(W)}\right] \\
&\leq \mathbf{Pr}\left[\text{distinct}(W) < (1 - \delta)\mu\right] \cdot 1 \\
&\quad + \mathbf{Pr}\left[\text{distinct}(W) \geq (1 - \delta)\right] \\
&\quad \cdot \mathbf{E}\left[\frac{\text{rare}(W, \alpha)}{\text{distinct}(W)} \,\middle|\, \text{distinct}(W) \geq (1 - \delta)\mu\right] \\
&\leq \varepsilon + \frac{1}{(1 - \delta)\mu} \cdot \mathbf{E}\left[\text{rare}(W, \alpha) \,\middle|\, \text{distinct}(W) \geq (1 - \delta)\mu\right] \quad (4.11) \\
&\leq \varepsilon + \frac{\mathbf{E}\left[\text{rare}(W, \alpha)\right]}{(1 - \delta)^2 \mu} = \varepsilon + \frac{P_\alpha}{(1 - \sqrt{2(\ln 1/\varepsilon)/\mu})^2 \mu}. \quad (4.12)
\end{aligned}
$$

If distinct$(W) < (1 - \delta)\mu$, rare$(W, \alpha)/$distinct$(W) \leq 1$ holds. Otherwise, we have: rare$(W, \alpha)/$distinct$(W) \leq$ rare$(W, \alpha)/((1 - \delta)\mu)$. Thus, Equation (4.11) holds. Moreover, let X denote a random variable, $X \geq 0$. Let e denote an event and $\neg e$ denote a situation that event e does not happen. Clearly, we have

$$\mathbf{E}\left[X \mid e\right] = \left(\mathbf{E}\left[X\right] - \mathbf{E}\left[X \mid \neg e\right] \cdot \mathbf{Pr}\left[\neg e\right]\right)/\mathbf{Pr}\left[e\right] \leq \mathbf{E}\left[X\right]/\mathbf{Pr}\left[e\right]. \tag{4.13}$$

Now, we define e as an event that distinct$(W) \geq (1 - \delta)\mu$, and X as rare(W, α). Thus, $\mathbf{Pr}\left[e\right] \geq 1 - \delta$ and Equation 4.12 holds.

Hence, Let ρ_α^L denote a lower bound of ρ_α, $\rho_\alpha^L = P_\alpha/m$, while ρ_α^U denote an upper bound of ρ_α, $\rho_\alpha^U = \varepsilon + \frac{P_\alpha}{(1 - \sqrt{2(\ln 1/\varepsilon)/\mu})^2 \mu}$. Algorithm 20 illustrates how to handle top-rarity query. Initially, we compute the upper and lower bounds for each α (lines 1–5). Symbol $\rho_{\max}^L$ is the threshold for all bounds. If there only exists

---

Algorithm 20 getTopRarity()

1: Generate a hash table H by Algorithm 17;
2: Compute the values of $\{P_\alpha\}$ by visiting H, where $1 \leq \alpha \leq g$;
3: **for** $(\alpha = 1$ to $g)$ **do**
4:     Compute the upper and lower bounds of ρ_α, denoted as ρ_α^U, and ρ_α^L;
5: **end for**
6: Let $\rho_{\max}^L = \max_{1 \leq \alpha \leq g}(\rho_\alpha^L)$;
7: **if** (there only exists one α such that $\rho_\alpha^U > \rho_{\max}^L$) **then**
8:     **return** α;
9:     **else**
10:     **for** (each α, $1 \leq \alpha \leq g \wedge \rho_\alpha^U > \rho_{\max}^L$) **do**
11:         Create an array B by Algorithm 18 and then compute ρ_α by Equation 4.5;
12:     **end for**
13:     **return** $\operatorname{argmax}_\alpha(\rho_\alpha)$;
14: **end if**

---

one α such that $\rho_\alpha^U < \rho_{\max}^L$, we can decide whether α is the result or not. Otherwise, we need to compute the exact ρ_α of all candidates by Algorithm 18.

4.5 Experimental Results

All codes were written in C++ and the experiments were conducted on a system with Intel Core 2 CPU (2.2GHz) and 2G memory. The synthetic and real datasets are described below.

- **Syn-R-S**: This data stream contains S tuples. Each tuple is an integer randomly selected from $[1, R]$. The probability of each tuple is randomly selected from $(0, 1)$.
- **IIPStream**: We gather all of records from the IIP dataset from 2001 to 2008 and result in 29,440 sighting records for 17,763 distinct icebergs, which means some icebergs are observed more

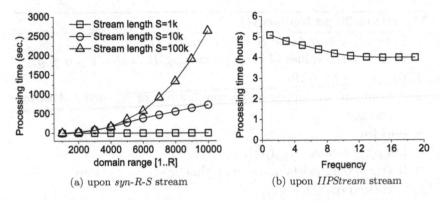

(a) upon *syn-R-S* stream   (b) upon *IIPStream* stream

Fig. 4.2   Time cost upon the synthetic and real data streams

than once.[2] Each record has an attribute to report the confidence of the sighting data, including R/V, VIS, RAD, SAT-LOW, SAT-MED, SAT-HIGH, and EST. We convert these confidence levels to 0.8, 0.7, 0.6, 0.5, 0.4, 0.3, and 0.4 respectively.

We first evaluate the time- and space-complexities of the exact solution. Figure 4.2(a) uses *Syn-R-S* data stream. The x-axis represents R, varying from 1,000 to 10,000, and the y-axis is the processing time cost. Let $\alpha = 1$. The processing time is mainly decided by the number of distinct elements in the data stream. When R or S grows, the processing time cost also increases. Figure 4.2(b) uses *IIPStream* data stream. When α increases, the time cost decreases slightly, because (i) most entries in B are non-zero when $\alpha = 1$, and (ii) most entries in B are zero when $\alpha > 0$ since most elements occur once in this stream.

Figure   4.3   demonstrates   the   space   consumption.   By Equation (4.4), when $i > j$, $B[i][j] = 0$ always holds. Thus, it is only necessary to maintain entries $B[i][j]$ in memory such that $i \leq j$. Figure 4.3(a) demonstrates the space consumption on *syn-R-S* data stream. Similar to Figure 4.2(a), the space consumption will increase when R or S grows. Figure 4.3(b) uses *IIPStream*. When α changes,

---

[2]See http://nsidc.org/data/g00807.html. Also see Section 2.5.

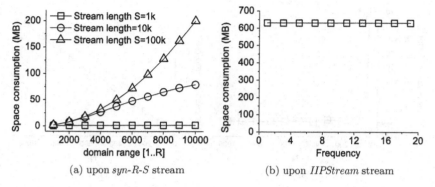

(a) upon *syn-R-S* stream   (b) upon *IIPStream* stream

Fig. 4.3 Space consumption upon the synthetic and real streams

the space consumption changes little, because the size of B, which dominates the space consumption, remains unchanged.

We next evaluate the approximate solution over the *IIPStream* data stream. In all tests, $\alpha = 1$. In Figure 4.4(a), we plot the Mean Squared Error (MSE) of the α-uncertain rarity approximation. When the number of the possible world instances N grows, the MSE value decreases. The precision is high since MSE is below 1.0×10^{-7} even when N is set to 25, a quite small value. Figures 4.4(b) and 4.4(c) demonstrate the space consumption and time cost under different N values. The time cost is approximately linear to N since more possible worlds are required. The space consumption almost remains unchanged when N grows from 100 to 1,000 since the size of the hash table is far greater than C. The executing cost is more efficient than the exact solution. Compared with Figures 4.2(b) and 4.3(b), the time cost and space consumption of the approximate solution are less than 0.01% and 0.1% of those of the deterministic solution respectively.

Finally, Figure 4.5 evaluates the performance of Algorithm 20 that computes top-rarity by pruning a part of frequencies. Let $filtering\ ratio = \frac{\#\text{frequencies filtered}}{\#\text{all frequencies}}$. Greater *filtering ratio* indicates better performance. Figure 4.5(a) demonstrates the track of *filtering ratio* when the threshold parameter ε is set to 0.001, 0.01, and 0.05 respectively. Upon almost all situations, *filtering ratio* is above 0.8. Moreover, the performance rises when ε decrements because the

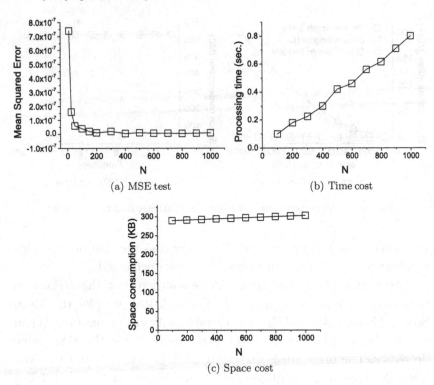

(a) MSE test

(b) Time cost

(c) Space cost

Fig. 4.4   Performance of the approximate solution upon *IIPStream* stream

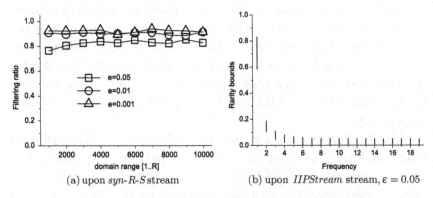

(a) upon *syn-R-S* stream

(b) upon *IIPStream* stream, $\varepsilon = 0.05$

Fig. 4.5   Top-rarity upon synthetic and real data streams

bound may be tighter on condition that μ is not small. Figure 4.5(b) demonstrates the bound for different frequencies where $\varepsilon = 0.05$. We get: $\rho^L_{\max} = 0.58$. Since ρ^U_1 is the only upper bound greater than $\rho^L_{\max}$, the top rarity is computed as 1. In other words, *filtering ratio* $= 1$.

Chapter 5

Set Similarity

5.1 Problem Definition

We model a probabilistic set A in a domain $\mathcal{D}$ as: $A = \{a_i : p_i | a_i \in \mathcal{D}, \forall i \in [1, n]\}$, where $\forall i \neq j$, $a_i \neq a_j$. Note that we require $p_i > 0$, as otherwise it can be trivially removed from the probabilistic set. The semantics is that each element a_i has an existential probability p_i, and the existence of the element is independent of each other. A probabilistic set is also shorten as a p-set. Although simple, it can model uncertainty in many applications. For example, [14] performs frequent itemset mining on uncertain transaction databases, where each "tuple" in the transaction database is a collection of items, each with its existential probability.

Under the *possible world* semantics, a probabilistic set A corresponds to many *possible worlds*, each containing a (certain) set which is a subset of the elements in A. Now consider similarity between two p-sets, A and B. Here we assume independence between the possible worlds of A and B. This assumption is reasonable in the absence of correlation between two p-sets, and it has been widely employed in other probabilistic database studies [25]. The comparison of two p-sets generates joint possible worlds, $PW(A, B)$, which are all the combination of possible worlds of individual p-sets, i.e., $PW(A, B) = PW(A) \times PW(B)$. The existential probability of $(pw_a, pw_b) \in PW(A, B)$ is $\mathbf{Pr}[pw_a] \cdot \mathbf{Pr}[pw_b]$.

For each possible world in $PW(A, B)$, a similarity value can be obtained. These values collectively form a discrete probabilistic distribution of similarity values, which fully characterizes the similarity between two p-sets.

A natural way to concisely capture the similarity by one single value is to use the mean of the similarities. Hence, we define *expected similarity* (*ES*) as follows.

Definition 5.1 (Expected Similarity, *ES*). The expected similarity between two p-sets, A and B, is the expected similarity between possible worlds of A and B, i.e.,

$$
\begin{aligned}
ES(A, B) &= \sum_{(pw_a, pw_b) \in PW(A,B)} sim(pw_a, pw_b) \cdot \mathbf{Pr}\left[(pw_a, pw_b)\right] \\
&= \sum_{pw_a \in PW(A) \wedge pw_b \in PW(B)} sim(pw_a, pw_b) \\
&\quad \cdot \mathbf{Pr}\left[pw_a\right] \cdot \mathbf{Pr}\left[pw_b\right],
\end{aligned}
\tag{5.1}
$$

where *sim* is a similarity function.

The choice of the similarity function, *sim*, depends on the application scenario. Here, we follow previous work [60] and focus on using Jaccard coefficient as the similarity function. The Jaccard coefficient between two sets is defined as their intersection size over their union size, i.e., $jac(X, Y) = \frac{|X \cap Y|}{|X \cup Y|}$. For simplicity, we define $sim(pw_a, pw_b) = 0$ when $pw_a = \emptyset$ and $pw_b = \emptyset$. Note that our methods can be generalized to other measures.

ES, being a concise summary, may not capture the overall distribution of similarity values [35]. We complement it with the notion of *confidence-based similarity*, or *CS*. We first define the *conditioned cumulative probability*, $\mathbf{CPr}(x, A, B)$, as the total probability associated with possible worlds where the similarity value is no less than x, i.e.,

$$
\mathbf{CPr}(x, A, B) = \sum_{(pw_a, pw_b) \in PW(A,B) \wedge sim(pw_a, pw_b) \geq x} \mathbf{Pr}\left[(pw_a, pw_b)\right].
\tag{5.2}
$$

Then, we define the confidence-based similarity as follows.

Definition 5.2 (Confidence-based Similarity, *CS*). Let *minconf* $\in [0,1]$ be a user-defined minimal confidence threshold. The *CS* between two *p*-sets, *A* and *B*, is the maximal similarity value x such that the corresponding cumulative probability is at least *minconf*, i.e., $CS(A, B, minconf) = \max\{ x \mid \mathbf{CPr}(x, A, B) \geq minconf \}$.

Example 5.1. Consider two *p*-sets *A* and *B* in Table 5.1. They have eight (joint) possible worlds, which are listed together with their similarities and existential probabilities in Table 5.1. For example, the 2nd possible world is made up of $\{2^A\}$ and $\{1^B, 2^B\}$. The former's existential probability is $(1 - 0.7) \cdot 1 = 0.3$, and the latter's existential probability is $1 \cdot 0.5 \cdot (1 - 0.8) = 0.1$. Therefore, the existential probability of the joint possible world is $0.3 \cdot 0.1 = 0.03$.

Example 5.2. We also show the similarity values of two *p*-sets in Table 5.2. The *ES* value is the average of Jaccard values in Table 5.1 weighted by their respective probabilities. The *CS* value for Jaccard similarity in the 2nd row is 0.5 because there are two possible worlds where the similarity is no less than 0.666 in Table 5.1; the total

Table 5.1 Possible Worlds and Similarities

(a) Example *p*-sets

A	B
$\{1 : 0.7, \ 2 : 1.0\}$	$\{1 : 1.0, \ 2 : 0.5, \ 3 : 0.8\}$

(b) All the joint possible worlds with non-zero probabilities (e^X is the element e of *p*-set X)

pw_a	pw_b	$\Pr(pw_a, pw_b)$	Jaccard
$\{2^A\}$	$\{1^B\}$	0.03	0
$\{2^A\}$	$\{1^B, 2^B\}$	0.03	0.5
$\{2^A\}$	$\{1^B, 3^B\}$	0.12	0
$\{2^A\}$	$\{1^B, 2^B, 3^B\}$	0.12	0.333
$\{2^A, 1^A\}$	$\{1^B\}$	0.07	0.5
$\{2^A, 1^A\}$	$\{1^B, 2^B\}$	0.07	1
$\{2^A, 1^A\}$	$\{1^B, 3^B\}$	0.28	0.333
$\{2^A, 1^A\}$	$\{1^B, 2^B, 3^B\}$	0.28	0.666

Table 5.2   Similarities of Two p-sets A and B

	Jaccard
$ES(A, B)$	0.44
$CS(A, B, minconf = 0.3)$	0.666
$CS(A, B, minconf = 0.5)$	0.333

probability of these possible worlds is: $0.07 + 0.28 = 0.35$ and hence is greater than the *minconf* $= 0.3$. In addition, it can be verified that this is the maximal value. For example, the total probability of possible worlds with a similarity greater than 0.666 is only 0.07.

We also observe that CS can give a more detailed picture of the similarity value distribution between two p-sets by varying the *minconf* value.

In many applications, we are mostly interested in highly similar results. Therefore, given a query p-set, we can define *expected similarity query* (ESQ) as finding all p-sets in a data stream such that the expected similarity between the query p-set and the result p-set is no less than a user-given threshold. We can define *confidence-based similarity query* (CSQ) in a similar fashion.

Although one may informally interpret the probabilities in our p-set model as weights, our similarity measures are fundamentally *different* from the *weight Jaccard* similarity [39], as the latter essentially only works on certain sets. For a simple example, consider $A = \{1 : 0.8\}$ and $B = \{1 : 0.4\}$. Weighted Jaccard will give similarity 0.5, while ES between the two is 0.32.

5.2 Exact Similarity Computation

In this section, we propose efficient methods to compute ES and CS between two p-sets exactly. The naïve method to compute these similarity values is based on their definitions, which needs to explore all possible world pairs from two p-sets, hence resulting in computational cost exponential in the size of the p-sets. The key observation to more efficient computational methods is the fact that our similarity functions only rely on a few key statistics, and these statistics can be computed efficiently via dynamic programming, and hence avoid the exponential cost of enumerating all possible worlds. In the following content, we will introduce the overall method first, and then give further details.

Overview. We can partition the joint possible worlds of A and B according to *equivalent classes* based on their intersection and union sizes. Specifically, we use $H[i, j]$ to denote the total existential probabilities of possible worlds (pw_a, pw_b) where pw_a and pw_b's intersection size is exactly i and their union size is exactly j, i.e.,

$$H[i, j] = \sum_{(pw_a, pw_b) \in PW(A,B) \wedge |pw_a \cap pw_b| = i \wedge |pw_a \cup pw_b| = j} \mathbf{Pr}\,[pw_a] \cdot \mathbf{Pr}\,[pw_b].$$

$$(5.3)$$

Example 5.3. Consider again the 16 possible worlds in Table 5.1. We regroup them into six classes, as shown in Table 5.3. Then it is easy to calculate $H[i, j]$, as shown in Table 5.4. For example, $H[1, 3]$ corresponds to the third and fourth possible worlds in Table 5.3. So $H[1, 3] = 0.12 + 0.28 = 0.4$.

Table 5.3 Equivalent Classes

pw_a	pw_b	$\Pr(pw_a, pw_b)$	i	j	Jaccard
$\{2^A\}$	$\{1^B\}$	0.03	0	2	0
$\{2^A\}$	$\{1^B, 3^B\}$	0.12	0	3	0
$\{2^A\}$	$\{1^B, 2^B, 3^B\}$	0.12	1	3	0.333
$\{2^A, 1^A\}$	$\{1^B, 3^B\}$	0.28	1	3	0.333
$\{2^A\}$	$\{1^B, 2^B\}$	0.03	1	2	0.5
$\{2^A, 1^A\}$	$\{1^B\}$	0.07	1	2	0.5
$\{2^A, 1^A\}$	$\{1^B, 2^B, 3^B\}$	0.28	2	3	0.666
$\{2^A, 1^A\}$	$\{1^B, 2^B\}$	0.07	2	2	1

Table 5.4 $H[i, j]$

	$j = 0$	$j = 1$	$j = 2$	$j = 3$
$i = 0$	0	0	0.03	0.12
$i = 1$	—	0	0.1	0.4
$i = 2$	—	—	0.07	0.28

Once $H[i,j]$ is calculated, we can calculate ES and CS easily as follows. For ES, we simply compute the weighted average of all the entries in H, i.e., $ES = \sum_{i=1}^{k} \sum_{j=i}^{m+n-k} H[i,j] \cdot (i/j)$, where k is the number of common elements. For CS, a naïve method is to sort all entries of H by decreasing order of similarity values (i.e., $\frac{i}{j}$), and then scan the sorted entries until the prefix sum of the probabilities is at least *minconf*.

When *minconf* is large, it is expected that only a few entries need to be summed up. We can calculate CS more efficiently by accessing entries in decreasing order of the similarity values and stop whenever the answer is found. The algorithm is described in Algorithm 21. We use a max heap that can return entries with the maximal similarity values. First, we push all the "diagonal" entries into the heap, as they have the maximal similarity value of 1.0 (lines 1–4). Then we repeatedly pop the entry with the maximal similarity, sum up the total probabilities, and break the loop if the current total probability is no smaller than *minconf* (lines 5–11). Finally, we push the "right" neighbor of the current entry into the heap. This is because, this "right" neighbor has the larger similarity than the "above" neighbor (since $\frac{i}{j+1} > \frac{i-1}{j}$).

The time complexity of Algorithm 21 is $O(k + out \cdot \log k)$, where $k \leq \min(n, m)$ is the number of common elements, and $out \leq k(n + m - k) - k(k - 1)/2$ is the number of entries that must be retrieved from the heap to calculate the CS value under a given *minconf*.

Computing H. Now we show that $H[i,j]$ can be computed in polynomial time via dynamic programming. Given normalized p-sets A and B, we construct an array $\vec{e} = (c_1, c_2, \ldots, c_k, d_1, d_2, \ldots, d_{m+n-2k})$ that collects all the elements from two p-sets. Consider the lth element (e_l). If it is a distinct element (i.e., $k < l \leq m+n-k$), then we use p_l to denote its associated probability in one of the p-sets. If e_l is a common element (i.e., $1 \leq l \leq k$), then we use p_l^X to denote its probability in p-set X.

Now we consider the sub-problem of calculating H where only the first l elements $(e_1, \ldots, e_l)$ and their associated probabilities are

---

Algorithm 21 Calculate CS from $H[i, j]$ ($H[i, j]$, *minconf*)

1: *heap* is a max-heap on the similarity values;
2: **for** $i = 1$ to k **do**
3:    *heap.push*$(1.0, i, i)$;
4: **end for**
5: $CPr \leftarrow 0$; $sim \leftarrow 0$;
6: **while** *heap*.empty $=$ **false do**
7:    $(sim, i, j) \leftarrow heap$.pop;
8:    $CPr \leftarrow CPr + H[i, j]$;
9:    **if** $CPr \geq minconf$ **then**
10:      **break**;
11:    **end if**
12:    **if** $j < m + n - k$ **then**
13:      *heap*.push$(\frac{i}{j+1}, i, j + 1)$;
14:    **end if**
15: **end while**
16: **return** sim;

---

considered. We denote the results as H^l. Obviously, $H^{m+n-k}[i, j]$ is the H we need.

If the current element e_l is a common element, then

$$H^l[i, j] = H^{l-1}[i, j](1 - p_l^A)(1 - p_l^B)$$
$$+ H^{l-1}[i, j - 1](p_l^A(1 - p_l^B) + (1 - p_l^A)p_l^B)$$
$$+ H^{l-1}[i - 1, j - 1]p_l^A p_l^B. \tag{5.4}$$

The above recurrence equation corresponds to the four possible cases regarding the occurrence of e_l in A and B, respectively. For example, the first part is for the case where e_l does not appear in either A or B; therefore, in this case, $H^l[i, j] = H^{l-1}[i, j](1 - p_l^A)(1 - p_l^B)$.

If the current element is a distinct element, then

$$H^l[i, j] = H^{l-1}[i, j](1 - p_l) + H^{l-1}[i, j - 1]p_l. \tag{5.5}$$

The above recurrence equation corresponds to the two possible cases regarding the occurrence of e_l.

Initially, we set $H^0[i,j] = 1$ when $i = 0 \wedge j = 0$, and $H^0[i,j] = 0$ otherwise. We also return $H^{l-1}[i,j] = 0$ if one of the following conditions is violated: (i) $0 \leq i \leq k$; (ii) $i \leq j \leq l \leq n + m - k$.

In this way, the dynamic programming-based algorithm based on Equations (5.4) and (5.5) is straightforward. We note that the method is actually a special case of the marginal vector convolution method [69] on a semi ring with $S = Z_{\max(n,m)}$.

Assuming $n \geq m \geq k$, the time complexity of computing $H^{m+n-k}[i,j]$ $(0 \leq i \leq k$ and $0 \leq j \leq m + n - k)$ can be shown to be $\Theta(kn^2)$ or $O(n^3)$, and the space complexity is $\Theta(kn)$, or $O(n^2)$.

5.3 Upper Bounds for Set Similarity

The goal of computing the upper bounds for a pair of p-sets is to prune such p-set pairs with similarity definitely smaller than a pre-defined threshold efficiently. Our upper bound calculation only requires two simple statistics, namely, the *expected set intersection size and union size*, which can be computed in $O(n + m)$ time due to linearity of expectation. First, the *expected size of a p-set* A, $\mathbf{E}[|A|]$, is $\sum_{pw \in PW(A)} |pw| \cdot \mathbf{Pr}[pw] = \sum_{l=1}^{n} p_l^A$. Second, the *expected intersection size of two p-sets A and B*, $\mathbf{E}[|A \cap B|]$, is $\sum_{(pw_a, pw_b) \in PW(A,B)} |pw_a \cap pw_b| \cdot \mathbf{Pr}[(pw_a, pw_b)] = \sum_{l=1}^{k} p_l^A \cdot p_l^B$. Last, the *expected union size of two p-sets A and B*, $\mathbf{E}[|A \cup B|]$, is $\mathbf{E}[|A|] + \mathbf{E}[|B|] - \mathbf{E}[|A \cap B|] = \sum_{l=1}^{k}(p_l^A + p_l^B - p_l^A \cdot p_l^B) + \sum_{l=k+1}^{n+m-k} p_l$.

The upper bound for *ES*. The *ES* value of two p-sets A and B is the expected Jaccard similarity between two random possible worlds of A and B, respectively. Hence, its value should be concentrated around the expected set intersection size over the expected set union size of A and B under certain conditions.

We first introduce the following lemma and then apply it to obtain an upper bound of the *ES* value. The core idea is that if a random variable X is the sum of *Poisson trials*, we can use the Chernoff bound to bound the total probabilities that its value deviates much from its expectation. Note that the set intersection size and union size are both sums of Poisson trials. For example, random variable $|A \cap B|$ can be deemed as the sum of performing k

coin tosses, each with $p_i^A p_i^B$, which is the probability that ith common element in A and B appears at the same time.

Lemma 5.1. *Let X and Y denote two sums of Poisson trials. $Y \geq X \geq 0$. Then $\mathbf{E}\left[X/Y\right] < UB_1(\mathbf{E}\left[X\right], \mathbf{E}\left[Y\right])$ where*[1]

$$UB_1(u, v) = \min_{\exp(-u/3)\leq\epsilon\leq 1}\left(2\epsilon + \frac{u + \sqrt{-3u\ln\epsilon}}{v - \sqrt{-2v\ln\epsilon}}\right). \qquad (5.6)$$

Proof. We define two events, H_1 and H_2, for X and Y. H_1 : $X > (1 + \lambda_X)\mathbf{E}\left[X\right]$. H_2 : $Y < (1 - \lambda_Y)\mathbf{E}\left[Y\right]$. For any ϵ satisfying $\exp(-\frac{\mathbf{E}[X]}{3}) \leq \epsilon \leq 1$, we set $\lambda_X = \sqrt{\frac{-3\ln\epsilon}{\mathbf{E}[X]}}$ and $\lambda_Y = \sqrt{\frac{-2\ln\epsilon}{\mathbf{E}[Y]}}$. Applying the Chernoff inequality, we have

$$\mathbf{Pr}\left[H_1\right] < \exp\left(-\frac{\lambda_X^2\mathbf{E}\left[X\right]}{3}\right) = \epsilon,$$

$$\mathbf{Pr}\left[H_2\right] < \exp\left(-\frac{\lambda_Y^2\mathbf{E}\left[Y\right]}{2}\right) = \epsilon.$$

Then, $\mathbf{E}\left[X/Y\right] = V_1 + V_2 + V_3 < 2\epsilon + \frac{1+\lambda_X}{1-\lambda_Y} \cdot \frac{\mathbf{E}[X]}{\mathbf{E}[Y]}$, where

$$V_1 = \mathbf{E}\left[X/Y \mid H_2\right] \cdot \mathbf{Pr}\left[H_2\right] < 1 \cdot \epsilon,$$

$$V_2 = \mathbf{E}\left[X/Y \mid H_1, \overline{H_2}\right] \cdot \mathbf{Pr}\left[H_1 \wedge \overline{H_2}\right] < 1 \cdot \epsilon,$$

$$V_3 = \mathbf{E}\left[X/Y \mid \overline{H_1}, \overline{H_2}\right] \cdot \mathbf{Pr}\left[\overline{H_1} \wedge \overline{H_2}\right] < \frac{(1 + \lambda_X)\mathbf{E}\left[X\right]}{(1 - \lambda_Y)\mathbf{E}\left[Y\right]} \cdot 1.$$

We will have the UB_1 function by expanding the definitions of λ_X and λ_Y and the theorem is proved. The range of ϵ in UB_1 is set because $\lambda_X, \lambda_Y \in [0, 1]^2$ and $e^{-u/3} > e^{-v/2}$. $\qquad\square$

---

[1] We assume $X/Y = 0$ when $Y = 0$.

[2] The upper bound of the Chernoff bound can be simplified as $\mathbf{Pr}\left[X\right] > (1 + \lambda)\mathbf{E}\left[X\right] < \exp\left(-\frac{\lambda^2\mathbf{E}[X]}{3}\right)$ when $0 \leq \lambda \leq 1$.

Unlike many common approaches where a value is obtained as an upper bound, our upper bound is the minimum value of a function. One can either choose an appropriate numerical analysis method to obtain the minimum upper bound, or use an appropriate fixed ϵ value to obtain a loose upper bound.

Given two p-sets A and B, the random variables X and Y are defined as: $X = |A \cap B|$, $Y = |A \cup B|$. Then, the upper bound of $ES(A, B)$ is computed below.

$$ES(A, B) = \mathbf{E}\left[X/Y\right] < UB_1(\mathbf{E}\left[|A \cap B|\right], \mathbf{E}\left[|A \cup B|\right]). \qquad (5.7)$$

The upper bound for *CS*. We first introduce Lemma 5.2 and then apply it to our *CS* problem.

Lemma 5.2. *Let X and Y be two sums of Poisson trials. For a given $\alpha \in (0, 1]$, if $\mathbf{E}\left[X\right] \leq \alpha \mathbf{E}\left[Y\right]$, we have*

$$\mathbf{Pr}\left[X \geq \alpha Y\right] < UB_2(\mathbf{E}\left[X\right], \mathbf{E}\left[Y\right], \alpha), \qquad (5.8)$$

where

$$UB_2(u, v, \alpha)$$
$$= \min_{u \leq \xi \leq \min(\alpha v, 2u)} \left(\exp\left(\frac{-(\alpha v - \xi)^2}{2\alpha^2 v} \right) + \exp\left(\frac{-(\xi - u)^2}{3u} \right) \right).$$
$$(5.9)$$

Proof. Consider the following two events, H_1 and H_2, where ξ is between $\mathbf{E}\left[X\right]$ and $\alpha \mathbf{E}\left[Y\right]$. $H_1 : X > \xi$. $H_2 : Y \leq \xi/\alpha$. Applying the Chernoff inequality, we have

$$\mathbf{Pr}\left[H_1\right] < \exp\left(-\frac{(\xi - \mathbf{E}\left[X\right])^2}{3\mathbf{E}\left[X\right]} \right) = \epsilon_1,$$

$$\mathbf{Pr}\left[H_2\right] \leq \exp\left(-\frac{(\alpha\mathbf{E}\left[Y\right] - \xi)^2}{2\alpha^2 \mathbf{E}\left[Y\right]} \right) = \epsilon_2,$$

$$\mathbf{Pr}\left[X \geq \alpha Y\right] = \mathbf{Pr}\left[(X \geq \alpha Y) \wedge (X \leq \xi)\right]$$
$$+ \mathbf{Pr}\left[(X \geq \alpha Y) \wedge (X > \xi)\right]$$
$$\leq \mathbf{Pr}\left[\xi \geq \alpha Y\right] + \mathbf{Pr}\left[X > \xi\right] < \epsilon_2 + \epsilon_1.$$

Hence, we have the UB_2 function by expanding the definitions of ϵ_1 and ϵ_2, and the theorem is proved. The range of ξ is because $\xi \in [\mathbf{E}\,[X]\,,\alpha\mathbf{E}\,[Y]]$ and $\xi \leq 2\mathbf{E}\,[X]$. $\qquad\square$

Given two p-sets A and B, we define two random variables X and Y as: $X = |A \cap B|$, $Y = |A \cup B|$. Applying Lemma 5.2, we have:

$$\mathbf{Pr}\left[\frac{|A \cap B|}{|A \cup B|} \geq \tau\right] < UB_2\left(\mathbf{E}\,[|A \cap B|]\,,\mathbf{E}\,[|A \cup B|]\,,\tau\right). \qquad (5.10)$$

Note that the CS value decreases monotonically with *minconf*. Hence if the confidence upper bound obtained by the UB_2 function is smaller than *minconf*, we can safely conclude that CS of A and B is strictly smaller than τ. In other words, if (i) $\mathbf{E}\,[|A \cap B|] \leq \tau \cdot \mathbf{E}\,[|A \cup B|]$, and (ii) $UB_2(\mathbf{E}\,[|A \cap B|]\,,\mathbf{E}\,[|A \cup B|]\,,\tau) \leq minconf$, then $CS(A, B) \leq minconf$.

5.4 Exact Streaming Approach

Given that we can compute the ES and CS similarities efficiently using dynamic programming-based algorithms, the naïve query processing algorithm to answer ESQ or CSQ queries is to compute the respective similarity between the query p-set and each p-set in the data stream one by one and output only those that pass the similarity threshold.

The obvious disadvantage of the basic query processing algorithm is that it needs to run a costly similarity computation algorithm for *every* p-set in the data stream irrespective of the similarity threshold. In fact, the efficiency can be improved by using the upper bounds for both ES and CS queries, as shown in Algorithm 22.

5.5 Approximate Streaming Approach

We devise approximate solutions to compute these queries yet with strong probabilistic guarantees.

Pairwise estimation of ES. The basic idea is to randomly sample $\lceil (\ln \frac{2}{\delta})/(2\epsilon^2) \rceil$ joint possible worlds (where ϵ and δ refer to the error threshold and confidence parameter respectively) and use the average

---

Algorithm 22 Exact Streaming solution $(Q, \{O_i\}, \tau, minconf)$

1: **for** each arriving p-set O_i **do**
2:      $pruned \leftarrow$ **false**;
3:      **if** the query type is ESQ **then**
4:          $ub \leftarrow$ Computer the upper bound by using Equation 5.6;
5:          Update $pruned \leftarrow$ **true** if $ub < \tau$;
6:      **else if** the query type is CSQ **then**
7:          $ub \leftarrow$ Computer the upper bound by using Equation 5.9;
8:          Update $pruned \leftarrow$ **true** if $ub < minconf$;
9:      **end if**
10:     **if** $pruned =$ **false then**
11:         $sim \leftarrow$ the similarity value between Q and O_i;
12:         Output O_i if $sim \geq \tau$;
13:     **end if**
14: **end for**

---

of the similarity in the sampled possible worlds to approximate the expected similarity ES. We have the following guarantee of the approximate similarity computed by this method. Let the similarity computed by the method mentioned above be $\widehat{ES}$, and let ES be the exact ES value. According to Hoeffding bound, we have: $\mathbf{Pr}\left[\left|\widehat{ES} - ES\right| \leq \epsilon\right] \geq 1 - \delta$.

The time complexity of this method is $O(n \cdot \epsilon^{-2} \ln \delta^{-1})$ and space complexity is $O(n)$, assuming $n \geq m$ [33].

Pairwise estimation of CS. We randomly generate G groups of possible worlds, and each group contains M pairs of possible worlds from A and B. For any ϵ, δ, we set $G = 24 \cdot \lceil \ln \frac{1}{\delta} \rceil$, $M = \lceil 2\epsilon^{-2} \rceil$. In each group, we select the $(minconf \cdot M)$-th largest similarity value into an array sa. Finally, we select the median value from G entries in the sa array. Let the similarity computed by the method mentioned above be $\widehat{CS}$, and let CS^- and CS^+ be the exact CS values with the minimum confidence $(minconf + \epsilon)$ and $(minconf - \epsilon)$ respectively, i.e., $CS^+ = CS(A, B, minconf - \epsilon)$, $CS^- = CS(A, B, minconf + \epsilon)$. We have: $\mathbf{Pr}\left[CS^- \leq \widehat{CS} \leq CS^+\right] \geq 1 - \delta$.

The space consumption is $O(\epsilon^{-2} + \ln\frac{1}{\delta})$, since we compute the similarity value group by group and each group contains $O(\epsilon^{-2})$ samples. Selecting of the k-largest value from an unsorted array of size n can be performed in $O(n)$ in a QuickSort-style algorithm. Therefore, the time complexity is $O(n \cdot \epsilon^{-2}\ln\delta^{-1})$, assuming $n \geq m$ [33].

Overall framework. Based on the above analysis, we devise the approximate streaming solution. Let Q denote the query p-set. For each arriving p-set O_i, we then generate a number of joint possible world instances based on Q and O_i. Once the similarity is no less than the pre-defined threshold, O_i is output.

5.6 Experimental Results

We report the results and analysis of the proposed probabilistic set model and similarity query processing algorithms. All programs were implemented in Java, and were conducted on a Window PC with an Intel Pentium IV 2.8GHz CPU and 4GB memory.

We use both synthetic and real-world datasets.

- **SYNα-U** and **SYNα-G.** These are the synthetic p-sets generated as follows: we form a p-set by randomly sampling α elements (without replacement) from a large universe of elements; each element is associated with a probability value generated from one of the following two distributions:

  — a Uniform distribution within the range of $[v, 0.9]$ with a default v value of 0.2.
  — a Gaussian distribution $N(\mu, \sigma)$ capped to the range of $(0, 1]$. By default, $\mu = 0.8$ and $\sigma = 0.2$.

  The resulting datasets are denoted as SYNα-U and SYNα-G, respectively.

- **pDBLP.** Automatic research profile construction is an essential step in applications such as expert finding, and is a nice feature to have for bibliography search engines. A basic profile is presented in a probabilistic way as $\langle p_1, p_2, \ldots, p_n \rangle$ where p_i quantifies the probability that a person is an expert in one of the n knowledge areas [13].

While different methods to model and estimate the probabilities have been proposed [13], we use a fairly simple yet effective method based on topical terms used in authors' DBLP entries.[3] Specifically, we extract, tokenize, and preprocess the publication titles of an author to get a *raw profile*, which is a *multiset* of terms. Globally, we select 1,000 general terms as possible descriptions of research interests. We construct each author's probabilistic profile as follows: (i) We remove terms not in the globally selected 1,000 terms; (ii) For the remaining term e, we convert the frequency of the term $c(e)$ into its probability $p(e)$ by adapting the sigmoid function as $p(e) = \frac{2}{1+\exp(-c(e))} - 1$. Similar transformations have been used to convert the numerical values (such as SVM classifier's output) to probability values [61].

Finally, we select the 5,000 most prolific authors and their probabilistic profiles as our pDBLP dataset.

- **pDeli.** We also use the social bookmarking dataset which was crawled from the Del.icio.us web site during 2006 and 2007. We obtain more than 23 million annotations from the original dataset by removing users and urls that occurred less than 10 times. We then map each tag to a set of urls to which the tag was used as part of a user's annotation. We associate with each url a probability value, which reflects the possibility or plausibility that the tag is appropriate for the url by adapting the sigmoid function as $p(u) = \frac{2}{1+\exp(-c(u))} - 1$, where $c(u)$ represents frequency of url u. The final dataset contains 44,876 tags.

Some statistics of the real datasets are given in Table 5.5. We construct the queries as follows:

- For a p-set in SYNα-U (respectively SYNα-G), we generate a *controlled* query p-set by adding "noise" to the original p-set. We randomly remove γ percent of elements from the set, and

---

[3]http://dblp.uni-trier.de/xml/.

Table 5.5 Descriptive Statistics

Dataset	DB Size	*p*-set Min/Max/Avg Size
pDBLP	5,000	27/708/204.9
pDeli	44,876	50/293,214/453.2

then add the same amount of random elements from the universe. The generated noisy query *p*-set is denoted as SYNα-U-Nγ (respectively SYNα-G-Nγ). All experimental results on the SYN dataset are averaged over 10 runs.

Unless otherwise specified, the default parameter settings are: $minconf = 0.5$ (for CS), $\tau = 0.5$, $\alpha = 1000$, $\gamma = 10\%$, $\epsilon = 0.06$, $\delta = 0.06$, $v = 0.2$, $\sigma = 0.2$, and $\mu = 0.8$.

We take the following measures: (i) **Memory Usage** is the total amount of memory used by an algorithm. (ii) **Computation Time** is the elapsed time to compute an ES or CS value using either exact or approximate method. (iii) **Query Time** is the query execution time per query for a collection of ESQ or CSQ queries. **Pruning time** is the time used by the pruning methods. (iv) **Candidate size** is the number of *p*-sets in the database that survive the pruning, and **result size** is the number of *p*-sets in the data stream that satisfy the query condition, i.e., the number of true positives. (v) **Pruning rate**. Given a query and a data stream containing N *p*-sets, let the candidate size be C, and let T be the number of *p*-sets in the data stream that does *not* satisfy the query condition. Pruning rate is defined as $\frac{N-C}{T}$. Intuitively, pruning rate reaches 100% when all the true negative results are pruned. (vi) **Average precision** is a common metric in IR to evaluate retrieval effectiveness. It is the precision (i.e., the percentage of retrieved results that are relevant) at a fixed position k average over all the queries.

Computing Similarities Exactly. We first evaluate our exact algorithms to compute the ES or CS values between two *p*-sets. Figures 5.1(a) and 5.1(b) show the space consumption and computation time between SYN1000-U and SYN1000-U-N10%.

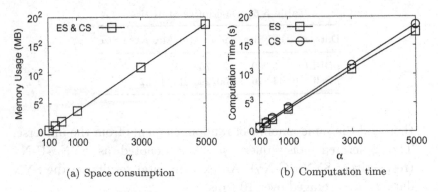

(a) Space consumption   (b) Computation time

Fig. 5.1   Exact similarity computation

Note that the time and space complexity is the same for other distributions. The exact solutions for *ES* and *CS* have similar space costs since they both need to maintain an *H* table in memory. We can see that the space cost increases quadratically with the increase of *p*-set size; time cost increases cubically with the increase of *p*-set size; both fit well with the theoretical prediction.

Computing Similarities Approximately. We evaluate our approximate similarity evaluation algorithms using SYN1000-G and SYN1000-G-N10%.

We first consider *ES* computation. We measure the Mean Squared Error (MSE) between the exact similarity values and values returned by our approximate methods. We plot MSE with respect to the number of samples (i.e., possible worlds) in Figure 5.2(a). As expected, the error reduces exponentially with the number of samples. On the other hand, the computational cost grows linearly with the sample size, as shown in Figure 5.2(b).

Next we show the MSE and computation time of the approximate algorithm for *CS* in Figures 5.2(c) and 5.2(d). We fix the number of groups to be 20, 50, and 80, and then vary the number of possible worlds within each group. As we can see, the error reduces exponentially with more possible worlds sampled; the error also reduces with more groups, although with a diminishing return. The computation time grows linearly with the number of groups and the number of samples within each group.

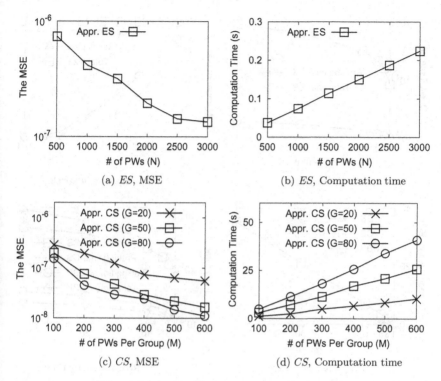

(a) *ES*, MSE

(b) *ES*, Computation time

(c) *CS*, MSE

(d) *CS*, Computation time

Fig. 5.2 Approximate similarity computation

Evaluating Pruning Efficiency on SYN. We report the performance of our pruning methods on synthetic datasets. We use SYN1000-G as the query and the database consists of 100 p-sets as SYN1000-G-Nγ ($\gamma = 1, 2, \ldots, 100$).

Figures 5.3(a) and 5.3(b) show the results for *ESQ*. Figure 5.3(a) shows the total query time and pruning time. The pruning time increases linearly with α, i.e., the p-set size, as the pruning cost is linear in the p-set size. Even when the p-set size is 5,000, the pruning time is only 54.4 milliseconds. The query time includes both the pruning and verification time. It first increases rapidly when the p-set size increases from 100 to 1,000; When the p-set size is above 1,000, the query time starts to increase slowly. This is mainly because: (i) The verification time using exact similarity evaluation is much larger than the time for pruning, as can be expected from their

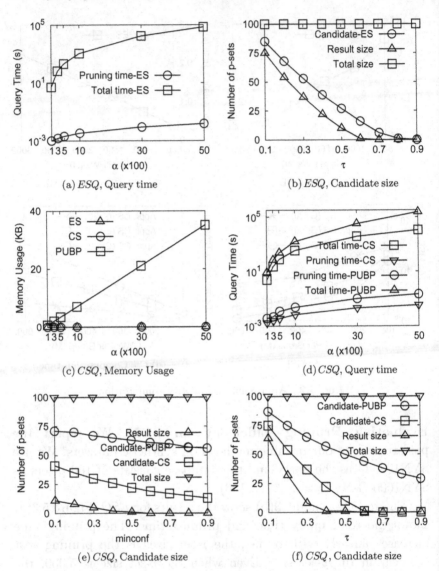

Fig. 5.3   Pruning effectiveness and efficiency on synthetic datasets

respective time complexities. It dominates the total time. (ii) The pruning rate becomes higher with the growth of the expected size of p-set, because both of our upper bounds become tighter with larger sets. When the p-set size is large enough, most of p-sets are pruned and hence the total time increases slowly.

Figure 5.3(b) shows the candidate size with varying similarity threshold τ. When τ increases, the result size decreases accordingly. The candidate size follows closely with the result size in all the cases. This is because our pruning is based on upper bound estimation and hence will always over-estimate the similarity by definition. The difference becomes negligible for $\tau > 0.7$.

Figures 5.3(c)–5.3(f) show the pruning efficiency for CSQ. In particular, we adapted the PUBP-based pruning approach proposed in [60] to our CSQ. Note that we incorporated the precomputation optimization into PUBP, which reduces its time from $O(n^2)$ to $O(n)$. Our method has a similar time complexity with PUBP. Here we will compare their computational costs and pruning rates in practice. Figures 5.3(c) and 5.3(d) show the space and time costs. Our method is immune to the growth of p-set, while PUBP needs to consume more. This is because our memory requirement is $O(1)$ while PUBP needs to load the precomputed cumulative probability vector into the memory, whose size is linear in α. In terms of query time, our method is much faster than PUBP-based method, although the pruning times of both methods are approximately the same. This is mainly because the number of candidate p-sets of our pruning is much less than that of PUBP-based pruning. We also show the candidate size of both pruning methods with respect to other parameters (*minconf* and τ) in Figures 5.3(e) and 5.3(f). It is obvious that our pruning is far more effective than PUBP in almost all cases. In particular, our candidate size follows the result size closely, where PUBP's candidate size is largely insensitive to the change of result size. For example, when $\tau \geq 0.4$, PUBP still returns about 60% of the data as candidates even if the result set is empty.

Performance on the pDBLP Dataset. We test our algorithms' performance on the pDBLP dataset. A sample of the queries and

Table 5.6 Sample Query Results on pDBLP

Query Author	Top-3 Similar Authors
Hanan Samet	Thomas Seidl, Walid G. Aref, Pavel Zezula
Jeffrey D. Ullman	Leonid Libkin, Yehoshua Sagiv, Richard J. Lipton
Michael I. Jordan	Zoubin Ghahramani, Eric P. Xing, John Shawe-Taylor

their top-3 most similar authors based on ES similarity are listed in Table 5.6. As we can see, the top-3 results are indeed researchers with closely matching research interest with the query author. For example, the first three rows contain well-known authors in the fields of spatial database, database theory, and machine learning.

Figures 5.4(a)–5.4(c) show the pruning rates with respect to various parameter settings for both types of queries if applicable. Note that PUBP pruning is only applicable to CSQ and hence should be compared with the CSQ curves. We can see that our pruning method outperforms PUBP substantially under all settings. For example, our pruning rate is close to 100% for $\tau \geq 0.4$, while PUBP's rate is only close to 100% when $\tau \geq 0.7$. The pruning rate of our method remains above 95% irrespective of the database size, while PUBP's rate increases with the database size. For both types of queries, our pruning rates increase with τ and DB size, and remain stable with *minconf*.

Figures 5.4(d)–5.4(f) show the query time with respect to various parameter settings. In Figure 5.4(d), we can see that for CSQ, the query time between our method and PUBP method is close when τ is small; the query time of our method drops quickly with the increase of τ, while PUBP's time decreases moderately; both query times reach their minimum and remain stable after τ is large enough. The time difference can be explained by the difference in pruning rates of the two methods (and hence the candidate size). Since verification cost is relatively more expensive than pruning cost, PUBP results in larger candidate set and this increases its time substantially. Figure 5.4(e) shows that the query time decreases when *minconf* increases, with our query time much faster than PUBP's. Figure 5.4(f) illustrates the scalability and trade-offs among algorithms using either exact or

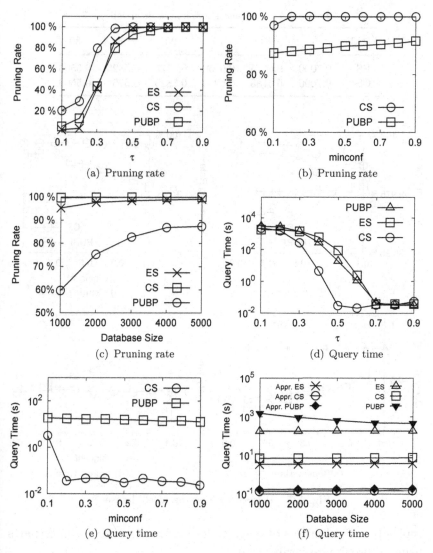

Fig. 5.4 Performance on the pDBLP dataset

approximate similarity calculation for verification. It can be seen that the overall query time hardly changes with the increase of the database size, thanks to relatively stable candidate size due to our pruning. The time cost using exact algorithm for verification is

Table 5.7　Average Precision@k on pDeli

AP@k	5	10	15	20	25	30
ES	0.7000	0.6675	0.6250	0.5875	0.5825	0.5500
CS	0.7000	0.6785	0.6280	0.5825	0.575	0.5500

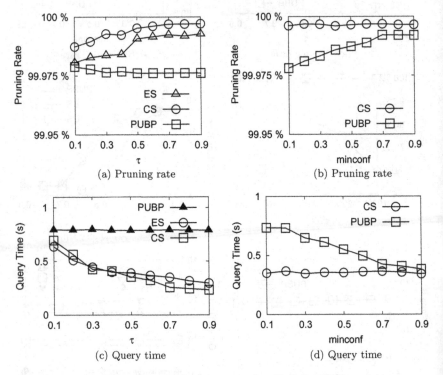

Fig. 5.5　Performance on the pDeli dataset

typically several orders of magnitudes higher than their counterparts using approximate verification.

Performance on the pDeli Dataset. We also test our algorithms' performance on the pDeli dataset that has very different characteristics from the pDBLP dataset: it is larger, more skewed (see Table 5.5), and sparser, since the number of unique elements (i.e., urls) is very large. Due to the large size of the p-sets, we use approximate methods for verification for all algorithms.

We select the url p-sets of twenty tags as queries to evaluate the effectiveness of *ESQ* and *CSQ*. We generate the ground-truth by asking five markers to label returned tags as relevant or not and tags that are labeled relevant by at least three markers are deemed as ground truth. Table 5.7 gives AP@k on pDeli.

We can see that both *ESQ* and *CSQ* achieve similarly good results in terms of AP@k; as the top-10 query results of *ESQ* and *CSQ* only contain few unrelevant tags, and even at 30th position, the average precisions of both queries are above 0.55. Note that due to the anonymization of the urls and lack of a complete context of tags, we expect our ground truth to be quite conservative and may miss some relevant tags. We can also see that the AP values between the two queries vary, with CS achieving a higher AP value than ES at position 10, but achieving a lower AP value than ES at position 20.

We plot pruning rates and query time for the algorithms with respect to different parameter settings in Figures 5.5(a)–5.5(d). Similar trends as those in the pDBLP dataset can be found too. Note that pruning rates for all algorithms are high mainly due to the sparseness of the dataset — only few tag pairs have common URLs. Nevertheless, our pruning methods outperform PUBP, and improve nicely with τ and remain stable with *minconf*. Note that PUBP is the pruning rule proposed in [60]. This also translates to the superiority of our query time over PUBP's under all parameter settings.

Chapter 6

Clustering

6.1 Problem Definition

Clustering aims at dividing a dataset into a number of clusters with inner-cluster distance minimized and inter-cluster distance maximized. For deterministic data, the distance between two tuples or two clusters is explicit, including Euclidean distance, Manhattan distance, and others. Note that SSQ is popular to measure the effectiveness of the clustering result. Let D denote a deterministic dataset, and $C_1, \ldots, C_k$ denote the central points of k clusters after employing a clustering method. The SSQ is defined as: $SSQ = \sum_{t \in D}(t - C(t))^2$, where $C(t)$ is the cluster center for tuple t, and $C(t) \in \{C_1, \ldots, C_k\}$. In general, a clustering method aims at minimizing the SSQ value.

In this chapter, we study the problem of clustering uncertain data streams in d-dimensional space over a sliding-window model that only considers the most recent W tuples in the data stream. Let $S = \{t_1, t_2, \ldots\}$ denote an uncertain data stream. Each tuple t_i has probability p_i to appear, $0 < p_i \leq 1$. The value of each tuple can also be imprecise, which is treated as a random variable drawn from a probability density function (PDF) f_i. Formally, each f_i has a region, $\mathsf{area}(t_i)$, $\forall z \notin \mathsf{area}(t_i)$, $f_i(z) = 0$, and $\int_{z \in \mathsf{area}(t_i)} f_i(z) = 1$.

Next comes the *distance* between two uncertain tuples, or two clusters. A simple definition is just using the distance between the corresponding central points. However, this definition cannot describe the real distance between two uncertain tuples accurately

[18], so the expected distance (ED) and the expected squared distance (ES) are used instead [18, 54, 66]. Let t_i and t_j be two uncertain tuples (with *attribute level uncertainty* only) and f_i, f_j be the corresponding probability density functions. ED and ES are defined below.

$$ED(t_i, t_j) \triangleq \int_{z_i \in \text{area}(t_i),\ z_j \in \text{area}(t_j)} \|z_i - z_j\| f_i(z_i) f_j(z_j)\, dz_i dz_j,$$

$$(6.1)$$

$$ES(t_i, t_j) \triangleq \int_{z_i \in \text{area}(t_i), z_j \in \text{area}(t_j)} (z_i - z_j)^2 f_i(z_i) f_j(z_j)\, dz_i dz_j.$$

$$(6.2)$$

ED and ES can be computed efficiently if some statistical information for each tuple is ready, including $E_{i,1}$ and $E_{i,2}$. Here, $E_{i,1}$ is a vector in d-dimensional space, and $E_{i,2}$ is a value, i.e., $E_{i,1} \in R^d$, and $E_{i,2} \in R$.

$$E_{i,1} = p_i \cdot \int_{z \in \text{area}(t_i)} z \cdot f_i(z)\, dz, \qquad (6.3)$$

$$E_{i,2} = p_i \cdot \int_{z \in \text{area}(t_i)} z^2 \cdot f_i(z)\, dz. \qquad (6.4)$$

Thus, ED and ES can be recomputed as below.

$$ED(t_i, t_j) = p_i p_j \cdot \left\| \frac{E_{i,1}}{p_i} - \frac{E_{j,1}}{p_j} \right\| = \|p_j \cdot E_{i,1} - p_i E_{j,1}\|,$$

$$ES(t_i, t_j) = \frac{E_{i,2}}{p_i} + \frac{E_{j,2}}{p_j} - 2 \cdot \frac{E_{i,1} E_{j,1}}{p_i p_j}.$$

Symmetrically, we define PSSQ (Probabilistic SSQ) as the uncertain version of SSQ to measure the effectiveness of the clustering result. Let $\{t_1, \ldots, t_N\}$ denote a set of N uncertain tuples, and $C(i) \in \{C_1, \ldots, C_k\}$ are the central points of k clusters. $PSSQ = \sum_{i=1}^{N} p_i \cdot ES(t_i, C(i))$, where $C(i)$ is the cluster center for tuple t_i and $C(i) \in \{C_1, \ldots, C_k\}$. Note that the discrete version of PSSQ is provided in [23]. The goal of an uncertain clustering method is to minimize PSSQ.

An interesting issue is how to compute the "central point" for a cluster of uncertain tuples. Undoubtedly, treating this point as the "center" will help to minimize the value of PSSQ. Let us consider a cluster $\{t_1, \ldots, t_m\}$. The PSSQ value is computed below, where C is the central point.

$$
\begin{aligned}
PSSQ &= \sum_{i=1}^{m} p_i \cdot ES(t_i, C) \\
&= \sum_{i=1}^{m} E_{i,2} - 2 \left(\sum_{i=1}^{m} E_{i,1} \right) \cdot C + \left(\sum_{i=1}^{m} p_i \right) \cdot C^2 \\
&= \sum_{i=1}^{m} E_{i,2} + \sum_{j=1}^{d} \left(\left(\sum_{i=1}^{m} p_i \right) \cdot C^{(j)} \cdot C^{(j)} \right. \\
&\quad \left. - 2 \left(\sum_{i=1}^{m} E_{i,1}^{(j)} \right) \cdot C^{(j)} \right).
\end{aligned}
\tag{6.5}
$$

In Equation (6.5), $C^{(j)}$ and $E_{i,1}^{(j)}$ denote the jth entries in C and $E_{i,1}$ respectively. $C^{(1)}, \ldots, C^{(d)}$ are d independent variables. For each variable $C^{(j)}$ (also denoted as x), assuming $a = \sum_{i=1}^{m} p_i$ and $b = \sum_{i=1}^{m} E_{i,1}^{(j)}$, it is convenient to verify that $\min(ax^2 - 2bx) = -\frac{b^2}{a}$ when $x = \frac{b}{a}$. Hence, since the PSSQ is minimized when: $\forall j, 1 \le j \le d$, we have $C^{(j)} = \frac{\sum_{i=1}^{m} E_{i,1}^{(j)}}{\sum_{i=1}^{m} p_i}$.

After putting all together, $C = \frac{\sum_{i=1}^{m} E_{i,1}}{\sum_{i=1}^{m} p_i}$, and the PSSQ is $\sum_{i=1}^{m} E_{i,2} - \frac{\left(\sum_{i=1}^{m} E_{i,1} \right)^2}{\sum_{i=1}^{m} p_i}$.

Clustering Feature. Here, we review Clustering Feature, a representative way to summarize a cluster of deterministic points. BIRCH [79] is an efficient data clustering method that is designed to incrementally cluster multidimensional metric data points in a data stream or dynamic environment. Consider a d-dimensional data space. Let $\{x_i\}$ denote a cluster of N deterministic data points, where $i = 1, 2, \ldots, N$. $x_i \in \mathbb{R}^d$. The centroid $(\overrightarrow{C})$ (note that $\overrightarrow{C}$ is denoted as $\overrightarrow{X0}$ in [79]), the root mean square distance from centroid (R), and the root square distance between all pairs of points (D) of a cluster $\{x_i\}$ are given as follows.

$$\vec{C} = \frac{\sum_{i=1}^{N} x_i}{N},$$

$$R = \left(\frac{\sum_{i=1}^{N} (x_i - \vec{C})^2}{N} \right)^{\frac{1}{2}},$$

$$D = \left(\frac{\sum_{i=1}^{N} \sum_{j=1}^{N} (x_i - x_j)^2}{N(N-1)} \right)^{\frac{1}{2}}.$$

Definition 6.1. (Definition 4.1 in [79]) The Clustering Feature (**CF**) of a cluster $\{x_i\}$ is defined as a triple: $\mathbf{CF} = (N, \vec{LS}, SS)$, where N is the number of data points in the cluster, $\vec{LS}$ is the linear sum of the N data points, i.e., $\sum_{i=1}^{N} x_i$, and SS is the square sum of N data points, i.e., $\sum_{i=1}^{N} x_i^2$.

CF summarizes statistical information about a cluster, based on which the above statistics can be computed directly. Moreover, **CF** has additive property. Assume $\mathbf{CF}_i = (N_i, \vec{LS}_i, SS_i)$ and $\mathbf{CF}_j = (N_j, \vec{LS}_j, SS_j)$ are *CF*s of two disjoint clusters, $\{x_i\}$ and $\{x_j\}$, respectively. The **CF** of a merged cluster, $\{x_i\} \cup \{x_j\}$, is computed as $(N_i + N_j, \vec{LS}_i + \vec{LS}_j, SS_i + SS_j)$.

BIRTH maintains an in-memory height-balanced tree of **CF**, called CF-tree, to cluster a massive dataset. A group of points close to one another is summarized by a *CF* and inserted into the CF-tree. Moreover, two or more *CF*scan be merged to save overall memory space. Finally, it is convenient to find clusters from a CF-tree.

Example 6.1. Figure 6.1 illustrates a small example with a sequence of 7 tuples, $t_1, t_2, \ldots, t_7$, in 2D space. The region of each tuple is a point: $(1.8, 3.6)$, $(1.8, 2.4)$, $(0.6, 3.0)$, $(4.2, 1.0)$, $(4.2, 2.2)$, $(3.0, 1.6)$ and $(1.8, 1.5)$ respectively.

First, we treat all tuples as the deterministic tuples. At time 6, the first six tuples are divided into two clusters, $C_1 = \{t_1, t_2, t_3\}$ and $C_2 = \{t_4, t_5, t_6\}$. It is not hard to compute the cluster features, $CF(C_1)$ and $CF(C_2)$, for these two clusters.

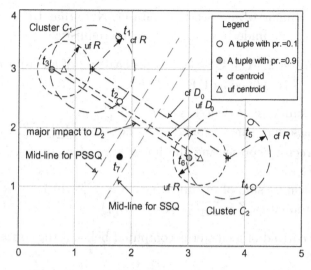

Fig. 6.1 *CF* vs. *UF*

$CF(C_1) = (3, (4.2, 9), 34.56)$. $CF(C_2) = (3, (11.4, 4.8), 52.68)$. The centroids of the two clusters are $(1.4, 3.0)$ and $(3.8, 1.6)$ respectively, indicated by crosses $(+)$. Clearly, to minimize the SSQ value, tuple t_7 should join C_1 since it is to the left side of the "mid-line for SSQ". Note that any point located on the "mid-line for SSQ" has the same distance to two centroids (indicated by crosses).

Second, we treat all tuples as the uncertain tuples with *existential uncertainty* (0.1 or 0.9). The existence confidences of t_3 and t_6 are significantly higher than the rest. At time 6, the first six tuples are also divided into two same groups. However, the centroids change to $(0.8, 3.0)$ and $(3.2, 1.6)$, indicated by triangles $(\triangle)$. The new centroids are much closer to t_3 and t_6 than before. Similarly, we also draw a line between the two centroids (indicated by triangles), namely "mid-line for PSSQ". Clearly, tuple t_7 should join C_2 since it is to the right side of the "mid-line for PSSQ".

6.2 Uncertain Feature

The popular use of Clustering Feature comes from the convenience of computing sophisticated statistical information, either for a single cluster, or for a pair of clusters [79]. We propose Uncertain Feature

(*UF*) to summarize an uncertain dataset. Note that *UF* is the same as *CF* once the underlying dataset is deterministic.

Definition 6.2. The **UF** (Uncertain Feature) of a cluster of tuples $\{t_1, \ldots, t_m\}$ is defined as $\mathbf{UF} = (P, P2, \overrightarrow{L}, S, Z)$.

- P: the sum of confidences, i.e., $P = \sum_{i=1}^{m} p_i$.
- $P2$: the square sum of confidences, i.e., $P2 = \sum_{i=1}^{m} p_i^2$.
- $\overrightarrow{L}$: a vector representing the linear sum of m tuples, i.e., $\overrightarrow{L} = \sum_{i=1}^{m} E_{i,1}$.
- S: the square sum of m tuples, i.e., $S = \sum_{i=1}^{m} E_{i,2}$.
- Z: computed as $Z = \sum_{i=1}^{m} (p_i E_{i,2} - E_{i,1}^2)$.

The centroid of a cluster is computed below if the corresponding UF exists.

$$C = \frac{\overrightarrow{L}}{P}. \tag{6.6}$$

Important statistics of one cluster or a pair of clusters include root mean square distance from centroid (R) and root mean square distance between all pairs of points (D) for single cluster; centroid Euclidean distance (D_0), centroid Manhattan distance (D_1), average inter-cluster distance (D_2), average intra-cluster distance (D_3) and variance increase distance (D_4) for a pair of clusters. We extend them to uncertain data environments.

Intuitively, a high-confidence tuple provides greater contribution. Hence, the root mean square distance from centroid, R, is recomputed below.

$$R^2 = \frac{1}{P} \cdot \sum_{i=1}^{m} (p_i \cdot ES(t_i, C))$$

$$= \frac{1}{P} \cdot \left(\sum_{i=1}^{m} p_i \cdot \left(\frac{E_{i,2}}{p_i} - 2 \frac{E_{i,1}}{p_i} \cdot \frac{\overrightarrow{L}}{P} + \left(\frac{\overrightarrow{L}}{P} \right)^2 \right) \right) = \frac{S}{P} - \left(\frac{\overrightarrow{L}}{P} \right)^2. \tag{6.7}$$

Second, D represents the average pairwise distance within a cluster. A pair of uncertain tuples in a cluster do not co-exist all the time if any one tuple has existential uncertainty. Let $Pr_{i,j}$ denote the co-existing confidence of two independent tuples t_i and t_j, then, $Pr_{i,j} = p_i \cdot p_j$. Note that $Pr_{i,j}$ can be treated as the weight of expected square distance between t_i and t_j. Hence, D is recomputed below.

$$D^2 = \frac{\sum_{i=1}^{m} \sum_{j=1}^{m,i \neq j} Pr_{i,j} \cdot ES(t_i, t_j)}{\sum_{i=1}^{m} \sum_{j=1}^{m,i \neq j} Pr_{i,j}} = 2 \cdot \frac{P \cdot S - \vec{L}^2 - Z}{P^2 - P2}. \quad (6.8)$$

We next consider statistics between two clusters. The first cluster has m_1 tuples, $\{t_1, \ldots, t_{m_1}\}$, with C_1 as the centroid. The second cluster has m_2 tuples, $\{t_{m_1+1}, \ldots, t_{m_1+m_2}\}$, with C_2 as the centroid. $D_0 - D_4$ are recomputed below.

$$D_0 = ((C_1 - C_2)^2)^{\frac{1}{2}} = \left\| \frac{\vec{L}_1}{P_1} - \frac{\vec{L}_2}{P_2} \right\|,$$

$$D_1 = |C_1 - C_2| = \sum_{t=1}^{d} \left| \left(\frac{\vec{L}_1}{P_1} \right)^{(t)} - \left(\frac{\vec{L}_2}{P_2} \right)^{(t)} \right|,$$

$$D_2^2 = \frac{\sum_{i=1}^{m_1} \sum_{j=m_1+1}^{m_1+m_2} Pr_{i,j} \cdot ES(t_i, t_j)}{\sum_{i=1}^{m_1} \sum_{j=m_1+1}^{m_1+m_2} Pr_{i,j}}$$

$$= \frac{P_2 \cdot S_1 + P_1 \cdot S_2 - 2 \cdot \vec{L}_1 \cdot \vec{L}_2}{P_1 P_2},$$

$$D_3^2 = \frac{\sum_{i=1}^{m_1+m_2} \sum_{j=1}^{m_1+m_2,j \neq i} Pr_{i,j} \cdot ES(t_i, t_j)}{\sum_{i=1}^{m_1+m_2} \sum_{j=1}^{m_1+m_2,j \neq i} Pr_{i,j}}$$

$$= \frac{2(P_1 + P_2)(S_1 + S_2) - 2(\vec{L}_1 + \vec{L}_2)^2 - 2(Z_1 + Z_2)}{(P_1 + P_2)^2 - (P2_1 + P2_2)},$$

$$D_4 = \sum_{h=1}^{m_1+m_2} Pr_h \cdot ES(t_h - C_0)$$

$$- \sum_{i=1}^{m_1} p_i \cdot ES(t_i - C_1) - \sum_{j=m_1+1}^{m_1+m_2} p_j \cdot ES(t_j - C_2)$$

$$= \frac{(\vec{L}_1 P_2 - \vec{L}_2 P_1)^2}{P_1 P_2 (P_1 + P_2)}, \qquad \text{where } C_0 = \frac{\vec{L}_1 + \vec{L}_2}{P_1 + P_2}.$$

Example 6.2. The **UF** for Cluster C_1 in Figure 6.1 is $\mathbf{UF}_1 = (P, P2, \overrightarrow{L}, S, Z) = (1.1, 0.83, (0.9, 3.3), 10.944, 0)$. So, $C_1 = (0.8, 3.0)$, $R_1 = 0.53$, and $D_1 = 1.33$. The **UF** for Cluster C_2 is $\mathbf{UF}_2 = (P, P2, \overrightarrow{L}, S, Z) = (1.1, 0.83, (3.54, 1.76), 14.516, 0)$. So, $C_2 = (3.2, 1.6)$, $R_2 = 0.53$, and $D_2 = 1.33$. Moreover, statistics for two clusters are computed as: $D_0 = 2.78$, $D_1 = 3.8$, $D_2 = 2.88$, $D_3 = 2.59$, and $D_4 = 2.06$.

Additive and Subtractive Properties. Similar to *CF*, our *UF* also has additive and subtractive properties.

Property 6.1. (*Additive*) Let $\mathbf{UF}_1$ and $\mathbf{UF}_2$ denote the uncertain features for two disjoint clusters C_1 and C_2 respectively. The uncertain feature $\mathbf{UF}_{1,2}$ for $C_1 \cup C_2$ is computed as $\mathbf{UF}_{1,2} = \mathbf{UF}_1 + \mathbf{UF}_2$. In other words, each element in $\mathbf{UF}_{1,2}$ is the sum of the corresponding elements in $\mathbf{UF}_1$ and $\mathbf{UF}_2$.

This property implies that **UF** can be maintained incrementally. Let $\mathbf{UF}_1$ denote the uncertain feature for a cluster. If a new tuple t joins that cluster, we update $\mathbf{UF}_1$ as $\mathbf{UF}_1 \leftarrow \mathbf{UF}_1 + \mathbf{UF}(t)$, where $\mathbf{UF}(t)$ is a new uncertain feature constructed based on t.

Property 6.2. (*Subtractive*) Let $\mathbf{UF}_1$ and $\mathbf{UF}_2$ denote uncertain features for two clusters C_1 and C_2 respectively, $C_1 \supset C_2$. The uncertain feature $\mathbf{UF}_{1,2}$ for $C_1 - C_2$ is computed as $\mathbf{UF}_{1,2} = \mathbf{UF}_1 - \mathbf{UF}_2$, i.e., each element in $\mathbf{UF}_{1,2}$ is the difference of the corresponding elements in $\mathbf{UF}_1$ and $\mathbf{UF}_2$.

Given the above properties, we can devise new solutions to cluster uncertain streams.

Comparison with *CF* and *ECF*. Currently, *CF* and *ECF* are two major techniques to summarize a cluster. These techniques have different working environments. *CF* can only process deterministic data, while *ECF* can handle data with attribute-level uncertainty. In contrast, *UF* can handle both kinds of uncertainties.

6.3 Extending the Existing Methods

The sliding-window model only considers the most recent W tuples in the data stream, but it is impossible to keep all such tuples in memory when W is huge. Instead, a succinct synopsis data structure (far smaller than the stream volume) that represents W tuples is maintained in the memory [10]. As tuples expire, it is challenging to update the synopsis data structure accordingly.

CluStream algorithm is a typical streaming algorithm that handles data points by using a series of *snapshots* in a *"pyramid"* framework [4], where a snapshot is a collection of *micro-clusters* (described by *CF*s) built upon all tuples from the start time to the current time. Recall that snapshots are stored in a tilted manner in the *pyramid* framework, thus recent snapshots are saved in the system more frequently. Based on these snapshots, clustering results can be computed easily. For example, if we have two snapshots at time i and j respectively, $i < j$, the clustering result for tuples in $(i, j]$ can be obtained as the difference of these two snapshots [4].

UMicro clusters an evolving data stream [5]. Initially, the maximal number of *micro-clusters* in the buffer is pre-defined. As the process continues, old micro-clusters will be removed if the buffer is full, and new micro-clusters are generated based on new tuples if they cannot be absorbed by any existing micro-cluster.[1] In this way, the buffer always contains the latest micro-clusters. When a clustering request comes, the result is computed based on micro-clusters in the buffer.

However, these two methods cannot be applied to the sliding-window model directly. In *CluStream*, snapshots are saved very frequently, so that the total space consumption is large. The infeasibility of *UMicro* comes from two aspects. First, the number of tuples created in the micro-clusters will change significantly under different data distributions. If most tuples can be absorbed by the

---

[1] We call a tuple *absorbed* by a micro-cluster only if it joins in the micro-cluster.

existing micro-clusters successfully, the number of tuples evolved rises. Otherwise, this value may be quite small because the existing micro-clusters are removed frequently. Second, *UMicro* drops the least recently updated micro-cluster when the buffer is full, but this policy does not necessarily drop the best one. For example, an "old" micro-cluster will become very "young" after absorbing a new tuple.

We attempted to devise *CluStream-SW* and *UMicro-SW* approaches based on *CluStream* and *UMicro* to handle the sliding-window model after utilizing the following framework.

Let n denote a small integer, and B denote a buffer for micro-clusters described by *CF*s. When a new tuple arrives, the micro-clusters in B are maintained continuously as *CluStream* or *UMicro*, respectively. At time points $l = \frac{W}{n}, \frac{2W}{n}, \ldots$, a copy of the snapshot that contains all micro-clusters in B is saved in memory independently. At the same time, this framework tries to remove the snapshot generated at $t - W$ (if it exists) to save memory space. In this way, at most n copies of snapshots are stored in memory, based on which clustering results can be computed. Assume a clustering request comes at time l, we then begin to find the oldest snapshot in memory at time $\lceil \frac{(l-W) \cdot n}{W} \rceil \cdot \frac{W}{n}$ to compute the difference with all micro-clusters in B, which results in a number of micro-clusters based on tuples arriving in $(\lceil \frac{(l-W) \cdot n}{W} \rceil \cdot \frac{W}{n}, l]$. The main drawback of this framework is the significant space consumption. Let M denote the number of active micro-clusters; the total number of micro-clusters stored will reach $M \cdot n$.

Moreover, the following two heuristic rules help to further improve efficiency.

Heuristic rule 1 (compressing existing snapshots): The space consumption can be reduced after compressing the existing snapshots. Although any micro-cluster in B has a chance to absorb new tuples after a snapshot is stored in memory, only some micro-clusters actually absorb tuples because of data distribution. In other words, a micro-cluster may be stored in memory more than once. To save space, redundant micro-clusters can be removed safely.

Heuristic rule 2 (removing expired micro-clusters): The accuracy of the clustering result can be improved if the expired micro-clusters, in which all tuples are expired, are removed from B. In this way, the number of micro-clusters in B is reduced and newly arrival tuples have more chances to construct new micro-clusters, which improves the accuracy of clustering results.

6.4 cluUS: A Novel Solution

Uncertain Feature Histogram. We next describe our new approach, *cluUS*, to cluster uncertain streams in a sliding-window model. Initially, the whole data stream is divided into a number of intervals with length equal to W/n. So, the first interval is $[0, \frac{W}{n})$, and the ith interval is $[\frac{(i-1)W}{n}, \frac{i \cdot W}{n})$. It is convenient to generate a number of micro-clusters based on the points located in each interval, where these micro-clusters are represented by *UF*s. However, as analyzed above, the total number of micro-clusters in the current window is comparable to *CluStream-SW* and *UMicro-SW*. Consequently, we devise a novel structure, Uncertain Feature Histogram (*UFH*), to further summarize some disjoint *UF*s at different intervals. Let $M_1, \ldots, M_m$ denote m micro-clusters at different intervals, summarized by $\mathbf{UF}_1, \ldots, \mathbf{UF}_m$, respectively. Let $I(M)$ denote the interval No. for micro-cluster M. A *UFH* is defined as below.

Definition 6.3. A **UFH** (*Uncertain Feature Histogram*) for m disjoint uncertain features at different intervals, $\mathbf{UF}_1, \ldots, \mathbf{UF}_m$, is described as: $\mathbf{UFH} = (\widetilde{UF}, \overrightarrow{VI}, \overrightarrow{VP}, \overrightarrow{VP2})$.

- $\widetilde{UF}$: a **UF** that is the sum of $\mathbf{UF}_1 \cdots \mathbf{UF}_m$.
- $\overrightarrow{VI}$: a vector to describe the interval distribution, i.e., $\overrightarrow{VI}^{(i)} = I(M_i)$, where $1 \leq i \leq m$.
- $\overrightarrow{VP}$: a vector to describe the confidence distribution, i.e., $\overrightarrow{VP}^{(i)} = \mathbf{UF}_i : P$, where $1 \leq i \leq m$.
- $\overrightarrow{VP2}$: a vector to describe the square confidence distribution, i.e., $\overrightarrow{VP2}^{(i)} = \mathbf{UF}_i : P2$, where $1 \leq i \leq m$.

Here, $A:B$ means B is an entry of object A. Consequently, $\mathbf{UF}_i:P$ and $\mathbf{UF}_i:P2$ represent P and $P2$ of $\mathbf{UF}_i$. A **UFH** is easy to compute. $\widetilde{UF}$ is computed by applying *additive* property to $\{\mathbf{UF}_i\}$, while the others are vectors to describe data distributions. The space consumption of **UFH** is economical. The size of **UFH** is $O(m+d)$ since $\widetilde{UF}$ consumes $O(d)$ and each of the rest entries has m items. Contrarily, storing m independent UFs requires $O(d \cdot m)$, much greater than $O(m+d)$.

UFH can be used to estimate a subset of clusters. Let Ψ denote a subset of $\{M_1 \cdots M_m\}$, $|\Psi| \leq m$, and $\mathbf{UF}(\Psi)$ denote the uncertain feature for Ψ. We compute the proportion of "sum of confidences" and "square sum of confidences" for Ψ, denoted as ϕ_1 and ϕ_2. Remember that $\overrightarrow{VI}$ records the interval distribution, so,

$$\phi_1 = \left(\sum_{C_i \in \Psi} \overrightarrow{VP}^{(i)} \right) \Big/ (\text{UFH}:\widetilde{UF}:P), \qquad (6.9)$$

$$\phi_2 = \left(\sum_{C_i \in \Psi} \overrightarrow{VP2}^{(i)} \right) \Big/ (\text{UFH}:\widetilde{UF}:P2). \qquad (6.10)$$

$\mathbf{UF}(\Psi)$ is estimated as: $\mathbf{UF}(\Psi) = (P, P2, \overrightarrow{L}, S, Z) \approx (\widetilde{UF}:P \cdot \phi_1, \widetilde{UF}:P2 \cdot \phi_2, \widetilde{UF}:\overrightarrow{L} \cdot \phi_1, \widetilde{UF}:S \cdot \phi_1, \widetilde{UF}:Z \cdot \phi_2)$. Here, $\mathbf{UF}(\Psi):P$ and $\mathbf{UF}(\Psi):P2$ are accurate, while others are not. The values of $\mathbf{UF}(\Psi):\overrightarrow{L}$ and $\mathbf{UF}(\Psi):S$ are reflected by ϕ_1, because the values of $E_{i,1}$ and $E_{i,2}$ are reflected by p_i in Equations (6.3)–(6.4). Similarly, the value of $\mathbf{UF}(\Psi):Z$ is reflected by ϕ_2.

One issue of UFH is the tradeoff between the performance and the compression ratio. When a UFH covers more UFs, the space consumption can be improved, but the quality of $\mathbf{UF}(\Psi)$ is reduced at the same time (see Figure 6.4(d) later). So, it is better to use a *lifespan* parameter L to restrict the maximal number of UFs in UFH, i.e., $m \leq L$ in Definition 6.3.

There are five kinds of $UFHs$, including *dead, partly dead, grown-up, on-growing,* and *fresh* $UFHs$. A UFH becomes *dead* only if all UFs covered are invalid. Notice that a **UF** is treated as "invalid"

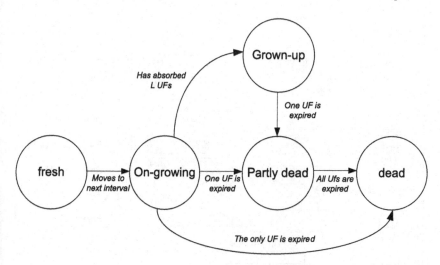

Fig. 6.2 The lifecycle of a *UFH*

if the corresponding interval is not fully inside the current window range. In a *partly dead UFH*, not all *UF*s are invalid. The remaining kinds of *UFH*s only contain unexpired *UF*s, including *grown-up*, *on-growing*, and *fresh UFH*s. A *grown-up UFH* contains L unexpired *UF*s without any **UF** at the current interval, which means that it cannot absorb new tuples. A *UFH* is *on-growing* if (i) one **UF** is at the current interval, or (ii) the number of *UF*s is smaller than L. Finally, as a special case of *on-growing UFH*, a *fresh UFH* only contains a single **UF**, located in the current interval. All kinds of *UFH*s are stored in B except *dead UFH*. Figure 6.2 illustrates the lifecycle of *UFH*.

Example 6.3. Figure 6.3 shows a small example with 9 *UFH*s in 1D space where $W = 40$, $L = 2$, $n = 4$. The size of an interval is $\frac{40}{4} = 10$. At time point t_c, the interval 1 is completely expired, 2 is partly expired, and the current interval is 6. In this paper, we call a *UF* at interval 2 "invalid" because a part of this interval is out of the current window range. We only consider the intervals 3–6. Clearly, UFH_1 is *dead* because all *UF*s are expired (at 1 and 2). In this way, UFH_4, UFH_6, and UFH_8 are *partly dead* because one of *UF*s is at

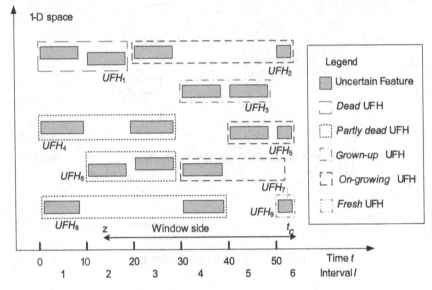

Fig. 6.3 An example of *UFH*

1 or 2, UFH_3 is *grown-up*, UFH_9 is *fresh*, and the rest (UFH_2, UFH_5, UFH_7) are *on-growing*.

Algorithm Description. *cluUS* (Algorithm 23) describes how to maintain micro-clusters continuously. It uses five input parameters, W, L, n, n_h and b, where W is the size of sliding window, L is the maximal lifespan of *UFH*, n is the number of intervals in the window range, n_h is the maximal number of *UFHs* stored in memory, and b represents the maximal number of *fresh UFHs*. The whole time span is divided into a number of equal-width intervals with the length equal to $\frac{W}{n}$.

Initially, the buffer B that stores all *UFHs* in memory is emptied (line 1). The maximal size of B is n_h. When a new tuple t arrives, it begins to compute the expected distance (*ED*, Equation (6.5)) between t and UFH', the closest *on-growing* or *fresh UFH* in B, so that the number of *UFs* in any *UFH* will not exceed L (line 3).

We then test whether t can be absorbed by UFH' or not. Generally, t is absorbed by UFH' only when it is very close to UFH'. However, how to formally define the term *"very close"* for a set

---

Algorithm 23 cluUS(W, L, n, n_h, b)

1: $B \leftarrow \emptyset$;
2: **for** each arriving tuple t **do**
3:     Find UFH', the closest *on-growing* or *fresh* UFH;
4:     **if** t lies inside the uncertainty boundary of UFH' **then**
5:       Add t to UFH';
6:     **else**
7:       Add a new UFH only contains one UF based on t into B;
8:       **if** there are $b + 1$ *fresh* UFHs **then**
9:         Merge one *fresh* UFH with the closest *on-growing* or *fresh* UFH;
10:       **end if**
11:     **end if**
12:   **if** $|B| > n_h$ **then**
13:     Remove a UFH from B with the smallest weight ω;
14:   **end if**
15:   **if** at the edge of an interval, i.e., $\frac{W}{n}, \frac{2W}{n}, \cdots$ **then**
16:     Remove *dead* UFHs from B;
17:   **end if**
18: **end for**

---

of tuples is still unclear. Instead, most work tends to describe the boundary of a cluster by using radius, i.e., two or three times of the radius to the centroid. This book uses $3R$ as the uncertain boundary. In other words, if $CED(t, C) \leq 3R$ where C and R are computed from $UFH' : \widetilde{UF}$ by Equations (6.6)–(6.7), t can be absorbed by UFH'. Otherwise, a new *fresh* UFH based on t must be created and added to B. To avoid generating too many UFHs in one interval, we use b to restrict the maximal number of *fresh* UFHs. If there are more than b fresh UFHs, we start to find the shortest distance between a pair of fresh UFHs or a fresh UFH and an on-growing UFH, so that this pair of UFHs are merged to reduce the number of fresh UFHs (lines 4–11).

When the buffer B is full, i.e., $|B| > n_h$, the most *"unimportant"* UFH is removed from B. The importance is based on two aspects.

First, young *UFH* is more important because (i) it will potentially absorb more tuples in the future, and (ii) it will stay in the window range for a long time. Here, the age of a *UFH* is decided by its oldest *UF*. Second, a heavier *UFH* (means larger $\widehat{UF}$:P) is often given more importance. After considering both aspects, the importance of a *UFH*, $\varphi(UFH)$, is defined as follows.

$$\varphi(UFH) = \sum_{\substack{1 \leq i \leq |\overrightarrow{VI}| }}^{|I_c - \overrightarrow{VI}^{(i)}| <= n} 2^{-\gamma \cdot (I_c - \overrightarrow{VI}^{(i)})} \cdot \overrightarrow{VP}^{(i)}. \qquad (6.11)$$

In the above equation, I_c is the current interval and γ is a user-defined half-decaying parameter. The importance of a **UF** is halved after $\frac{1}{\gamma}$ intervals. In addition, the importance of a **UF** is reset to zero if it is expired.

It is critical to protect some young *UFHs*; otherwise, they will be removed from B frequently even though they belong to new clusters. For example, a *fresh UFH* ($age(UFH) = 1$) often contains a small number of tuples, which makes $\varphi(UFH)$ small. Similarly, some young *on-growing UFHs* are also small. Here, $age(UFH) = I_c - I(UF') + 1$, where I_c is the current interval and UF' is the newest *UF* in *UFH*. For example, in Figure 6.3, $age(UFH_3) = 2$, $age(UFH_4) = 4$. To protect such *UFHs*, we measure the weight of a *UFH* according to the following rules, (i) the weight of a *fresh UFH* is set to ∞, higher than other kinds of *UFHs*, (ii) for an *on-growing UFH* satisfying $age(UFH) \leq L$, the weight is amplified by a radio $\frac{L}{age(UFH)}$, (iii) for the rest, the weight is equal to $\varphi(UFH)$. In conclusion, the weight of a *UFH*, $\omega(UFH)$, is defined below (lines 12–14).

$$\omega(UFH) = \begin{cases} \infty, & age(UFH) = 1; \\ \varphi(UFH) \cdot \dfrac{L}{age(UFH)}, & 1 < age(UFH) \leq L; \\ \varphi(UFH), & age(UFH) > L. \end{cases} \qquad (6.12)$$

Finally, *dead UFHs* are removed from B at the edge of an interval (lines 15–17).

Clustering On Demand. When a clustering request comes, results can be computed based on B. The *fresh, on-growing*, and *grown-up* UFHs are totally considered. For each *partly dead* UFH, only the unexpired part is considered. Next, a weighted k-means clustering algorithm is used to compute the final result [43].

Online Maintenance of $\omega(UFH)$: At line 13 of Algorithm 23, the UFH with the smallest weight $\omega(UFH)$ are removed if B is full. Computing $\omega(UFH)$ for all UFHs one by one consumes significant amounts of time. However, we can improve the process by maintaining an additional element φ for each UFH. When absorbing one tuple t_i, the corresponding φ is updated as: $\varphi \leftarrow \varphi + p_i$. At the edge of an interval, the elements φ of all UFHs are updated as follows.

$$\varphi = \begin{cases} 2^{-\gamma} \cdot \varphi, & \forall i, \overrightarrow{VI}^{(i)} \neq I_c - n + 1; \\ 2^{-\gamma} \cdot \varphi - 2^{-\gamma \cdot n} \overrightarrow{VP}^{(i)}, & \exists i, \overrightarrow{VI}^{(i)} = I_c - n + 1, \end{cases} \quad (6.13)$$

where I_c is the current interval.

Space- and time- complexities: *cluUS* is both space-efficient and time-efficient. At most n_h UFHs are stored in the buffer B. As analyzed above, the size of a UFH is $O(L+d)$, where L is the lifespan and d is the space dimension. Thus, the total space consumption is $O(n_h(L + d))$.

The main cost of processing a new tuple t is at lines 3, 9 and 13. To find the closest *on-growing* or *fresh* UFH to t, the cost of line 3 is $O(n_h \cdot d)$. At line 9, computing the shortest distance between a pair of fresh UFHs or a fresh UFH and an on-growing UFH to merge a pair of UFHs when there are $b + 1$ *fresh* UFHs costs $O(b \cdot n_h \cdot d)$. Fortunately, this step is used infrequently. At line 13, the UFH with the smallest ω is removed when B is full, so the cost is $O(n_h)$. As a result, the per-tuple processing cost is $O(n_h \cdot d)$.

6.5 Experimental Results

We implemented a series of experiments on real and synthetic datasets to evaluate *cluUS* algorithm with comparison to *CluStream-SW* and *UMicro-SW*. Written in C++, all codes run on an openSUSE system with an Intel Core2 Duo 2.33GHz CPU and 4GB memory.

Our testing plan consists of seven parts. First, we report the effects of parameter settings for *cluUS* algorithm. Second, we test the purity of *cluUS* in comparison with *CluStream-SW* and *UMicro-SW*, showing that *cluUS* is more accurate. Subsequently, we compare the per-tuple processing cost and space consumption among three approaches, showing that *cluUS* is more efficient. Fourth, we test the scalability of *cluUS* by varying dimension d and window size W. Fifth, we evaluate the performance by varying the perturbation rate. Sixth, we compare CF and UF, showing that CF cannot suit for uncertain data. Finally, we test the influence of the arriving order of *cluUS*.

Data sources. We used two kinds of datasets to test the performance. The first one is a real uncertain dataset, IIP.[2] from 1998 to 2010. It contains 62,582 records. We used two quantitative variables, the latitude and the longitude, for testing. Second, we also use three deterministic datasets, including one synthetic dataset and two real datasets. By using two perturbation policies mentioned later, they can be converted to uncertain datasets.

1. **Synthetic Dataset (Syn).** We constructed a 500,000-tuple, d-attribute synthetic stream with m drifting clusters as follows. The relative fraction of the data points belonging to each cluster is the same. Initially, we randomly selected m points in the unit cube as the seeds for all clusters, each moving along a direction in rate $\frac{1}{50,000}$, i.e., each seed travels 1 every 50,000 time points. The moving direction of each seed is randomly selected and will be reset every 50,000 time points. In addition, we also use a parameter l_i for each cluster i, where l_i is drawn from a uniform distribution in the range of $(0, 0.05)$ every 50,000 time points. At every time point, only one point is generated at one of the clusters with the position drawn uniformly from a cube centralized at the seed with l_i as the size along each dimension. We use *Syn-d-m* to

---

[2]http://nsidc.org/data/g00807.html.

describe a synthetic dataset containing m drifting clusters in d-D space.

2. **Network Intrusion Detection dataset (NID).**[3] Reported in KDD-CUP'99, the dataset consists of raw TCP connection records from a local area network over two weeks. Each record corresponds to either a normal connection or one of four attack types. All 34 continuous attributes are used to construct a data stream.

3. **Forest CoverType dataset (FCT).**[4] This dataset has 581,012 observations, each consisting of 54 attributes, including 10 quantitative variables, 4 binary wilderness areas, and 40 binary soil type variables. Here, all 10 quantitative variables are used to create a data stream.

Perturbation policy 1 (Attribute-level uncertainty): Let $\overrightarrow{\sigma}$ denote a vector of standard deviations of entire deterministic dataset D along all dimensions. For each tuple t_i in D, add normal distribution with mean equal to zero and a vector of standard variables $\overrightarrow{\sigma_i}$. Here, $\overrightarrow{\sigma_i}^{(j)}$, the jth entry in $\overrightarrow{\sigma_i}$, is randomly picked from $[0, \rho \cdot \overrightarrow{\sigma}^{(j)}]$, where $\overrightarrow{\sigma}^{(j)}$ is the jth entry in $\overrightarrow{\sigma}$ and ρ is a predefined *"perturbation rate"* parameter. Thus, $E_{i,1}$ and $E_{i,2}$ are computed as: $E_{i,1} = t_i$, $E_{i,2} = t_i^2 + \overrightarrow{\sigma_i}^2$ easily.[5] In other words, when ρ increases, $E_{i,1}$ will remain unchanged, but $E_{i,2}$ will probably increase.

Perturbation policy 2 (Existential uncertainty): We use two models to assign the occurrence probability of each tuple, inclusive of *uniform* and *exponential* distributions. In *uniform* distribution, the probability is drawn from uniform distribution in the range of $[0, 1]$. In *exponential* distribution, the probability p of each tuple is decided by a probability density function $F(p) = \lambda e^{-\lambda(1-p)}$. The default value of λ is 1. Note that the value of probability p must be re-assigned if it exceeds $[0, 1]$.

Both policies can be utilized at the same time. We name an uncertain dataset as $(D, attr, exis)$, where D is the underlying

---

[3]http://kdd.ics.uci.edu/databases/kddcup99/kddcup99.html.
[4]http://kdd.ics.uci.edu/databases/covertype/covertype.html.
[5]http://mathworld.wolfram.com/NormalDistribution.html.

deterministic dataset, *attr* is attribute-level perturbation, and *exis* is existential perturbation. For example, $(FCT, \text{n-0.01}, \text{e})$ is an uncertain dataset based on *FCT* with attribute-level perturbation (normal, $\rho = 0.01$) and existential perturbation (exponential distribution); $(Syn\text{-}20\text{-}10, \text{u})$ denotes an uncertain dataset based on *Syn-20-10* only with existential perturbation (uniform distribution).

Evaluating parameter settings. We study the input parameters of *cluUS* here. Figure 6.4(a) reports the track of per-tuple processing cost on four uncertain datasets by varying n_h. For other parameters, $(W, L, n, b, \gamma) = (5 \times 10^4, 5, 20, \frac{2n_h}{n}, \frac{1}{20})$. For *cluUS*, the per-tuple processing cost is mainly affected by deciding whether a new tuple t can be absorbed by any of candidate *UFHs* (line 3, Algorithm 23), which needs to compute the distances between t and

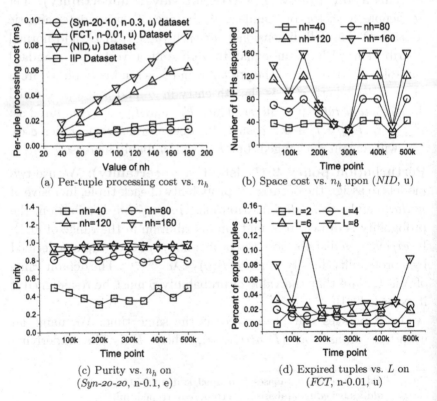

(a) Per-tuple processing cost vs. n_h (b) Space cost vs. n_h upon (NID, u)

(c) Purity vs. n_h on   (d) Expired tuples vs. L on
$(Syn\text{-}20\text{-}20, \text{n-0.1}, \text{e})$ $(FCT, \text{n-0.01}, \text{u})$

Fig. 6.4   Parameters evaluation on uncertain datasets

each candidate *UFH*. Here, the candidate *UFH*s refer to the *fresh* and *on-growing* *UFH*s. When n_h increases, *cluUS* tends to spend more time to process a new tuple because of more candidate *UFH*s. In addition, the per-tuple processing cost differs significantly over different data streams. For example, *cluUS* processes (*syn-20-10*, n-0.3, u) faster than the other datasets, since the number of candidate *UFH*s for the synthetic dataset is quite smaller than other datasets (refer to Figure 6.6(b) later).

Figure 6.4(b) illustrates the track of space consumption upon the dataset (NID, u) by varying n_h. The x-axis is the time point, and the y-axis describes the number of *UFH*s stored in B under different n_h. In general, the increment of n_h leads to more space consumption. The space consumption varies significantly at different time point. For example, during $(2 \times 10^5, 3 \times 10^5)$, only a small number of *UFH*s are stored, while during $(3.5 \times 10^5, 4 \times 10^5)$ the buffer is full. In fact, the number of *UFH*s in B is highly dependent on data distribution. If the new tuples do not differ a lot, most of them will be absorbed by the existing *UFH*s, making this number small. Moreover, most tuples arriving in $(2 \times 10^5, 3 \times 10^5)$ in *NID* belong to one category, *smurf DOS attack*.

Purity is important to measure the quality of the clustering result. Assume m clusters are denoted as $M_1, \ldots, M_m$. For any cluster M_i, the purity is defined as $\frac{P'(M_i)}{P(M_i)}$, where $P(M_i)$ denotes the sum of occurrence probabilities of tuples in M_i, and $P'(M_i)$ is the sum of occurrence probabilities of the largest classification in M_i. Because the weight of M_i is $\frac{P(M_i)}{\sum P(M_i)}$, the overall purity is computed as: $\sum \left(\frac{P'(M_i)}{P(M_i)} \cdot \frac{P(M_i)}{\sum P(M_i)} \right) = \frac{\sum P'(M_i)}{\sum P(M_i)}$. Figure 6.4(c) illustrates the track of purity upon (*Syn-20-20*, n-0.1, e). The value of n_h varies from 40 to 160. We find that purity is influenced by n_h. The clustering quality can be significantly improved if given more *UFH*s. When $n_h = 40$, the purity is around 50%. Contrarily, when n_h rises to 160, the purity is above 95%.

Parameter L in *cluUS* controls the maximal number of *UF*s in a *UFH*. As shown in Figure 6.2, if a *UFH* contains more than one *UF*, it is *half-dead* before turning *dead*, so that we can only "estimate" the *UF* for the unexpired tuples from a *half-dead UFH*, which reduces the quality. To provide higher quality, we hope to restrict the proportion of the expired tuples at a low level. Figure 6.4(d) shows the proportion of expired tuples also rises when L rises from 2 to 8. The proportion of expired tuples is small when $L = 2$ or 4. But when $L = 8$, this value may exceed 10%. In order to reduce the expired tuples in *UFH*s, it is better to use a small L. But a greater L makes a *UFH* absorb more tuples in different intervals. As a compromise, we use $L = 5$ in our tests below.

In the following experiments, $W = 50,000$. The parameters for *cluUS* are: $(L, n, n_h, b, \gamma) = (5, 20, 180, 18, \frac{1}{20})$. For *UMicro* and *CluStream*, the maximal number of micro-clusters is 180.

Effectiveness. We test the effectiveness of *cluUS* in terms of purity that is simple and transparent to measure a cluster. Figure 6.5(a) computes the average purity among different approaches upon four uncertain datasets. The average purity at y-axis is computed as the average value of *purity* obtained every 50,000 time points. For comparison purpose, we also computed the average purity under a *static* approach, which is actually k-means algorithm running upon all tuples in the window. The quality of the clustering result obtained by the three streaming approaches is close to that of the *static* approach. For (*FCT*, n-0.01, u) dataset, the quality is almost the same. Figure 6.5(b) also shows the purity of one uncertain dataset.

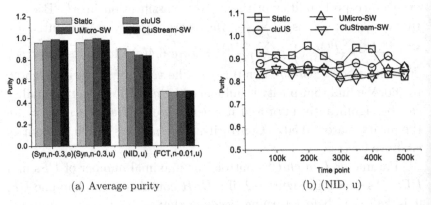

(a) Average purity   (b) (NID, u)

Fig. 6.5   Purity testing

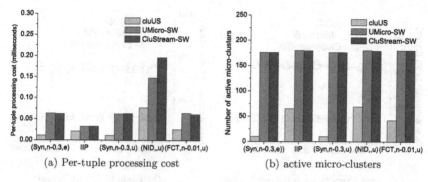

(a) Per-tuple processing cost   (b) active micro-clusters

Fig. 6.6 Per-tuple processing cost testing

Efficiency. Figure 6.6(a) shows the per-tuple processing cost of three approaches on four uncertain datasets. Obviously, *cluUS* runs significantly faster than the other two approaches. For all approaches, the per-tuple processing cost mainly focuses on searching the nearest micro-cluster to the new tuple. More candidate micro-clusters lead to greater per-tuple processing cost. As analyzed above, in *cluUS*, only *fresh* and *on-growing UFHs* can absorb new tuples, so the number is often smaller than the maximal size of the buffer. Contrarily, in *UMicro-SW* and *CluStream-SW* approaches, a new tuple can be absorbed by any micro-cluster stored in memory, which is considerably greater than *cluUS*. Figure 6.6(b) also illustrates the average number of candidate micro-clusters in different approaches. This value is quite small in *cluUS*.

Figure 6.7 compares space consumption. The difference is very significant. The other two approaches need nearly 10 times more space than *cluUS*, since many copies of snapshots are stored at the edge of intervals. In addition, the gap between *cluUS* and the other two approaches on the *IIP* dataset is narrower than other datasets, since the *IIP* dataset only has two attributes, while other datasets have at least 10 attributes.

Scalability. Figure 6.8 illustrates the effects of *cluUS* by varying d from 10 to 50. The purity remains high in all situations, while the per-tuple processing cost and space consumption are linear with the value of d, because the size of a micro-cluster will increase when d

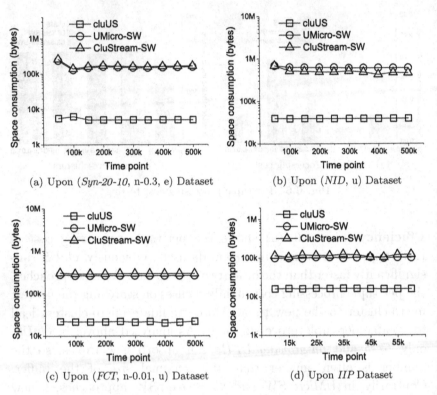

Fig. 6.7   The track of space consumption on uncertain datasets

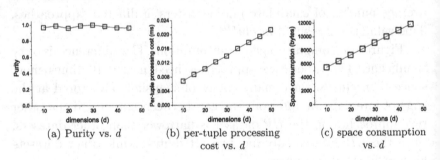

Fig. 6.8   Scalability of *cluUS* upon (*Syn-d-10*, n-0.3, u) by changing d

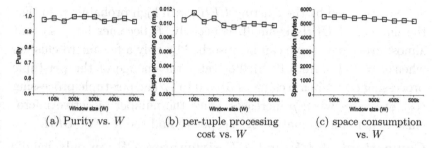

(a) Purity vs. W (b) per-tuple processing cost vs. W (c) space consumption vs. W

Fig. 6.9 Scalability of *cluUS* upon $(Syn\text{-}20\text{-}10,$ n-0.3, u$)$ by changing W

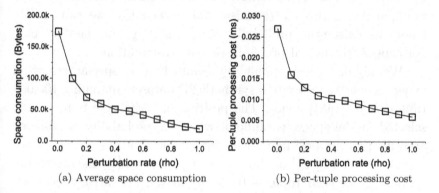

(a) Average space consumption   (b) Per-tuple processing cost

Fig. 6.10 The impact of perturbation rate

increases, which means *cluUS* needs to spend more time to find the nearest candidate micro-cluster in B for a new tuple.

Figure 6.9 describes the effect of *cluUS* by varying window size W from 50,000 to 500,000 upon a synthetic dataset containing 2,000,000 tuples. Under all situations, *cluUS* has similar performance.

Testing by varying perturbation rate. We use two perturbation policies to add existential and attribute-level uncertainties. Since the effect of the existential uncertainty has been illustrated through above experiments, Figure 6.10 only tests the effect of the attribute-level uncertainty.

Figure 6.10(a) illustrates the average space consumption when the perturbation rate ρ changes from 0 to 1. When ρ increases, the average space consumption continues to decrease, since a new tuple will be absorbed by the existing *UFHs* with high probability, so that the number of *UFHs* is small. Especially, R becomes large so that almost every new tuple can be absorbed by only a few micro-clusters when $\rho = 1$. Figure 6.10(b) illustrates the change of the per-tuple processing cost when ρ changes from 0 to 1. The per-tuple processing cost decreases when ρ increases, since the number of active micro-clusters is reduced, making it cheaper to find the nearest *UFH*.

Comparison of *CF* and *UF* structures. *CF* can only handle deterministic dataset [79]. A necessary step in applying *CF* to uncertain datasets is to remove the probabilistic information. For example, for a tuple with existential uncertainty, we can simply ignore its existential probability. Unfortunately, this method may not capture the actual probabilistic data distribution.

We highlight this point by conducting a special series of experiments. We generate a synthetic 2D dataset containing 100,000 tuples in [0,1]*[0,1] space. The position of each tuple is uniformly selected in the space in random, while the probability is assigned according to the position: (i) in the left and bottom area (i.e., the x-axis value is in $[0, \frac{1}{4}]$ or the y-axis value is in $[0, \frac{1}{4}]$), the existential probability of each tuple is 0.02, (ii) in the rest area, tuples are divided into nine cells equally, and the probability is decided by its distance to the cell center, i.e., the tuples close to the center are assigned a high probability (close to 1) and the tuples at edge are assigned small probabilities (close to 0). Figure 6.11(a) illustrates a sample set containing 1,500 points. Large points mean higher

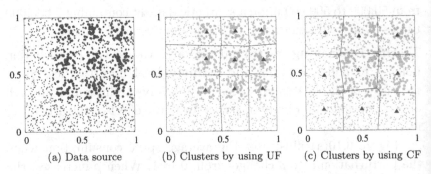

(a) Data source   (b) Clusters by using UF   (c) Clusters by using CF

Fig. 6.11   The comparison between *CF* and *UF*

probability, and small points mean low probability. Assuming the window size is 30,000, Figure 6.11(b) shows the results obtained by using *UF* structure. The cluster centers are still almost the centers of nine cells. Figure 6.11(c) illustrates the nine cluster centers obtained by using *CF* structure, ignoring the existential confidence. Obviously, this figure cannot represent the actual data distribution.

Testing the influence of the arriving order. So far, we have verified the effectiveness and efficiency of our algorithm if the streaming data arrives out of order. But in real applications, streaming data usually displays a trend since the data model may

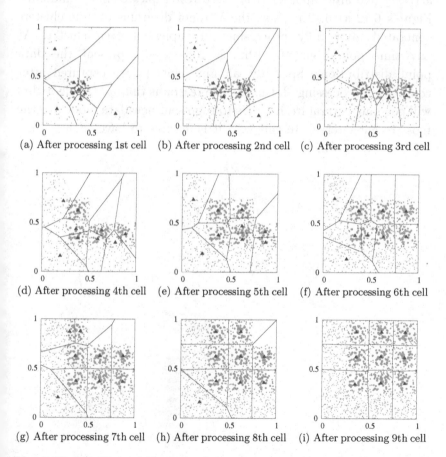

(a) After processing 1st cell   (b) After processing 2nd cell   (c) After processing 3rd cell

(d) After processing 4th cell   (e) After processing 5th cell   (f) After processing 6th cell

(g) After processing 7th cell   (h) After processing 8th cell   (i) After processing 9th cell

Fig. 6.12 The Voronoi diagrams of nine clusters upon an ordered data stream

change with time going on. Hence, it is critical to check the effectiveness of a clustering algorithm under such situation. Alex *et al.* have studied this issue in [8]. They use a synthetic dataset where each cluster appears one after another. When all tuples in each cluster have arrived, a Voronoi diagram for all tuples arriving so far is drawn for illustration. In this way, they show their patch clustering algorithm can handle this situation well.

Our algorithm (*cluUS*) is also capable of handling such kind of data streams. Figure 6.11(a) shows a stream of nine clusters in the top right area. Now, we assume the tuples in each cluster arriving one after another, while the rest tuples coming randomly. Figures 6.12(a)–6.12(i) show the Voronoi diagrams of nine clusters generated after fully processing all tuples in each cluster. At any time point, our algorithm is robust to represent the data point distributions. Specially, all nine clusters are captured after completing processing all tuples. The reason is that *cluUS* algorithm will generate several fresh *UFH*s to represent new data models in the most recent interval. In this way, it is feasible to have enough *fresh UFH*s to represent a new cluster.

Chapter 7

Conclusion

Nowadays, many applications need to handle *streaming* data, which is huge and arriving rapidly, such as sensor network, traffic monitoring and Internet. Different from traditional static database management systems (DBMS), the goal of streaming data management is to devise one-pass, space- and time-efficient solutions to implement specific querying and analyzing tasks. Moreover, data uncertainty also widely exists in such applications, i.e., each tuple in a stream may have *attribute-level* uncertainty, *existential* uncertainty, or both. The possible world model has been widely used in uncertain data management field. Dealing with an uncertain data stream is far more challenging than dealing with a deterministic data stream, due to the exponential growth of the possible world instances to the data volume.

We study several representative querying and mining tasks in this book, including top-k, rarity, set-similarity, and clustering. At first, we study how to deal with uncertain top-k queries. We design a general framework to deal with uncertain top-k queries upon the sliding-window model, which supports several top-k queries, such as PT-k, U-Top$k$, U-kRanks and Pk-Top$k$. We also propose solutions to deal with ER-Top$k$ query continuously by using some novel data structures. Second, we have taken the first step to study rarity in the uncertain data field. Besides a dynamic programming technique to obtain the precise result, an approximate algorithm is proposed with better efficiency. Third, we present a simple and computationally tractable model for uncertain sets where each element is associated with its existential probability, following which novel solutions are given to deal with this issue. Finally, we propose one efficient synopsis data structure, Uncertain Feature (*UF*), to summarize a cluster of uncertain tuples with attribute level and existential uncertainties at the same time, based on which *cluUS* algorithm is given to support the sliding-window model.

There still remain a lot of work to be done in future. First, how to deal with a general uncertain data model where both kinds of uncertainties exist, and tuples in the stream are dependent to each other. To study such a general model will make the issue much more complex. Hence, some research tend to work on a simple model, for example, the point uncertain model. How to devise efficient solutions to deal with a more complex model remains as a challenge.

The second future direction is to study time-sensitive model, such as sliding window. In general, sliding window model is much more difficult than the landmark model, since the existing tuples may expire after a certain period. So, processing sliding-window model is meaningful.

References

1. S. Abiteboul, P. Kanellakis, and G. Grahne. On the representation and querying of sets of possible worlds. *ACM SIGMOD Record*, 16(3):34–48, 1987.
2. C. C. Aggarwal. *Managing and Mining Uncertain Data.* Springer, New York, 2009.
3. C. C. Aggarwal. On high dimensional projected clustering of uncertain data streams. In *Proc. ICDE*, pages 1152–1154, 2009.
4. C. C. Aggarwal, J. Han, J. Wang, and P. S. Yu. A framework for clustering evolving data streams. In *Proc. VLDB*, pages 81–92, 2003.
5. C. C. Aggarwal and P. S. Yu. A framework for clustering uncertain data streams. In *Proc. ICDE*, pages 150–159, 2008.
6. C. C. Aggarwal and P. S. Yu. A survey of uncertain data algorithms and applications. *IEEE TKDE*, 21(5):609–623, 2009.
7. P. Agrawal, A. D. Sarma, J. Ullman, and J. Widom. Foundations of uncertain-data integration. *Proceedings of VLDB*, 3(1):1080–1090, 2010.
8. N. Alex, A. Hasenfuss, and B. Hammer. Patch clustering for massive data sets. *Neurocomputing*, pages 1455–1469, 2009.
9. N. Alon, Y. Matias, and M. Szegedy. The space complexity of approximating the frequency moments. In *Proc. STOC*, pages 20–29, 1996.
10. B. Babcock, S. Babu, M. Datar, R. Motwani, and J. Widom. Models and issues in data stream systems. In *Proc. PODS*, pages 1–16, 2002.
11. B. Babcock, M. Datar, R. Motwani, and L. O'Callaghan. Maintaining variance and k-medians over data stream windows. In *Proc. PODS*, pages 234–243, 2003.
12. B. Babcock and C. Olston. Distributed top-k monitoring. In *Proc. SIGMOD*, pages 28–39, 2003.

13. K. Balog and M. de Rijke. Determining expert profiles (with an application to expert finding). In *Proc. IJCAI*, pages 2657–2662, 2007.

14. T. Bernecker, H.-P. Kriegel, M. Renz, F. Verhein, and A. Züfle. Probabilistic frequent itemset mining in uncertain databases. In *Proc. ACM SIGKDD*, pages 119–128, 2009.

15. A. Chakrabarti, G. Cormode, and A. McGregor. Robust lower bounds for communication and stream computation. In *Proc. STOC*, pages 641–650, 2008.

16. A. Chakrabarti, T. Jayram, and M. Pǎtraşcu. Tight lower bounds for selection in randomly ordered streams. In *Proc. SODA*, pages 720–729, 2008.

17. V. Chandola, A. Banerjee, and V. Kumar. Anomaly detection: A survey. *ACM Computing Surveys*, 41(3):15, 2009.

18. M. Chau, R. Cheng, B. Kao, and J. Ng. Uncertain data mining: An example in clustering location data. In *Proc. PAKDD*, pages 199–204, 2006.

19. T. H. Cormen, C. E. Leiserson, R. L. Rivest, and C. Stein. Introduction to algorithms. *the MIT Press*, pages 265–268, 2001.

20. G. Cormode and M. Garofalakis. Sketching probabilistic data streams. In *Proc. SIGMOD*, pages 281–292, 2007.

21. G. Cormode, F. Korn, and S. Tirthapura. Exponentially decayed aggregates on data streams. In *Proc. ICDE*, pages 1379–1381, 2008.

22. G. Cormode, F. Li, and K. Yi. Semantics of ranking queries for probabilistic data and expected ranks. In *Proc. ICDE*, pages 305–316, 2009.

23. G. Cormode and A. McGregor. Approximation algorithms for clustering uncertain data. In *Proc. PODS*, pages 191–200, 2008.

24. G. Cormode, S. Tirthapura, and B. Xu. Time-decaying sketches for sensor data aggregation. In *Proc. ACM PODC*, pages 215–224, 2007.

25. N. N. Dalvi and D. Suciu. Efficient query evaluation on probabilistic databases. *VLDB Journal*, 16(4):523–544, 2007.

26. N. N. Dalvi and D. Suciu. Management of probabilistic data foundations and challenges. In *Proc. ACM PODS*, pages 1–12, 2007.

27. G. Das, D. Gunopulos, N. Koudas, and D. Tsirogiannis. Answering top-k queries using views. In *Proc. VLDB*, 2006.

28. M. Datar and S. Muthukrishnan. Estimating rarity and similarity over data stream windows. In *Proc. ESA*, pages 323–334, 2002.

29. A. Deshpande, C. Guestrin, S. Madden, J. M. Hellerstein, and W. Hong. Model-driven data acquisition in sensor networks. In *Proc. VLDB*, pages 588–599, 2004.

30. J. C. Dunn. A fuzzy relative of the isodata process and its use in detecting compact well-separated clusters. *Journal of Cybernetics*, 3:32–57, 1973.

31. M. Ester, H.-P. Kriegel, J. Sander, and X. Xu. A density-based algorithm for discovering clusters in large spatial databases with noise. In *Proc. KDD*, pages 226–231, 1996.

32. R. Fagin, A. Lotem, and M. Naor. Optimal aggregation algorithms for middleware. In *Proc. PODS*, 2001.

33. M. Gao, C. Jin, W. Wang, X. Lin, and A. Zhou. Similarity query processing for probabilistic sets. In *Proc. ICDE*, pages 913–924, 2013.

34. J. Ge, S. Zdonik, and S. Madden. Top-k queries on uncertain data: On score distribution and typical answers. In *Proc. ACM SIGMOD*, pages 375–388, 2009.

35. T. Ge and Z. Li. Approximate substring matching over uncertain strings. *Proceedings of VLDB*, 4(11):772–782, 2011.

36. T. J. Green and V. Tannen. Models for incomplete and probabilistic information. *IEEE Dat Engineering Bulletin*, 29(1):17–24, 2006.

37. S. Guha and A. McGregor. Approximate quantiles and the order of the stream. In *Proc. PODS*, pages 273–279, 2006.

38. S. Guha, R. Rastogi, and K. Shim. Cure: An efficient clustering algorithm for large databases. In *Proc. SIGMOD*, pages 73–84, 1998.

39. M. Hadjieleftheriou and D. Srivastava. Weighted set-based string similarity. *IEEE Data Engineering Bulletin*, 33(1):25–36, 2010.

40. M. Hua, J. Pei, A. W. C. Fu, X. Lin, and H.-F. Leung. Efficiently answering top-k typicality queries on large databases. In *Proc. VLDB*, pages 890–901, 2007.

41. M. Hua, J. Pei, W. Zhang, and X. Lin. Efficiently answering probabilistic threshold top-k queries on uncertain data. In *Proc. ICDE*, pages 1403–1405, 2008.

42. M. Hua, J. Pei, W. Zhang, and X. Lin. Ranking queries on uncertain data: A probabilistic threshold approach. In *Proc. SIGMOD*, pages 673–686, 2008.

43. A. Jain and R. Dubes. *Algorithms for Clustering Data*. Prentice Hall, New Jersey, 1998.

44. T. Jayram, S. Kale, and E. Vee. Efficient aggregation algorithms for probabilistic data. In *Proc. SODA*, pages 346–355, 2007.

45. T. Jayram, A. McGregor, S. Muthukrishnan, and E. Vee. Estimating statistical aggregates on probabilistic data streams. In *Proc. PODS*, pages 243–252, 2007.

46. S. R. Jeffery, M. Garofalakis, and M. J. Franklin. Adaptive cleaning for RFID data streams. In *Proc. VLDB*, pages 163–174, 2006.

47. J. Jestes, F. Li, Z. Yan, and K. Yi. Probabilistic string similarity joins. In *ACM SIGMOD*, pages 327–338, 2010.

48. C. Jin, M. Gao, and A. Zhou. Handling ER-Top$k$ query on uncertain streams. In *Proc. DASFAA*, pages 326–340, 2011.

49. C. Jin, K. Yi, L. Chen, J. X. Yu, and X. Lin. Sliding-window top-k queries on uncertain streams. *Proceedings of the VLDB Endowment*, 1(1):301–312, 2008.

50. C. Jin, K. Yi, L. Chen, J. X. Yu, and X. Lin. Sliding-window top-k queries on uncertain streams. *The VLDB Journal*, 19(3):411–435, 2010.

51. C. Jin, J. X. Yu, A. Zhou, and F. Cao. Efficient clustering of uncertain data streams. *Knowledge and Information Systems*, 40(3):509–539, 2014.

52. C. Jin, J. Zhang, and A. Zhou. Continuous ranking on uncertain streams. *Frontiers of Computer Science*, 6(6):686–699, 2012.

53. C. Jin, M. Zhou, and A. Zhou. Computing rarity on uncertain data. *Science China: Information Sciences*, 54(10):2028–2039, 2011.

54. B. Kao, S. D. Lee, D. W. Cheung, W.-S. Ho, and K. F. Chan. Clustering uncertain data using Voronoi diagrams. In *Proc. ICDM*, pages 333–342, 2008.

55. H.-P. Kriegel, P. Kunath, M. Pfeifle, and M. Renz. Probabilistic similarity join on uncertain data. In *DASFAA*, pages 295–309, 2006.

56. H.-P. Kriegel and M. Pfeifle. Density-based clustering of uncertain data. In *Proc. KDD*, pages 672–677, 2005.

57. H.-P. Kriegel and M. Pfeifle. Hierarchical density-based clustering of uncertain data. In *Proc. ICDM*, pages 689–692, 2005.

58. A. Kumar and C. Ré. Probabilistic management of ocr data using an rdbms. *Proceedings of the VLDB Endowment*, 5(4):322–333, 2012.

59. J. Li, S. Saha, and A. Deshpande. A unified approach to ranking in probabilistic databases. *Proceedings of the VLDB Endowment*, 2(1):502–513, 2009.

60. X. Lian and L. Chen. Set similarity join on probabilistic data. *Proceedings of the VLDB Endowmentg*, 3(1):650–659, 2010.

61. H.-T. Lin, C.-J. Lin, and R. C. Weng. A note on platt's probabilistic outputs for support vector machines. *Machine Learning*, 68(3):267–276, 2007.

62. V. Ljosa and A. K. Singh. Top-k spatial joins of probabilistic objects. In *Proc. ICDE*, pages 566–575, 2008.

63. K. Mouratidis, S. Bakiras, and D. Papadias. Continuous monitoring of top-k queries over sliding windows. In *Proc. ACM SIGMOD*, pages 635–646, 2006.

64. S. Muthukrishnan. *Data Streams: Algorithms and Applications.* Foundations & Trends in Theoretical Computer Science, 2005.

65. S. Nepal and M. V. Ramakrishna. Query processing issues in image (multimedia) databases. In *Proc. ICDE*, pages 22–29, 1999.

66. W. K. Ngai, B. Kao, C. K. Chui, R. Cheng, M. Chau, and K. Y. Yip. Efficient clustering of uncertain data. In *Proc. ICDM*, pages 436–445, 2006.

67. L. O'Callaghan, N. Mishra, A. Meyerson, and S. Guha. Streaming-data algorithms for high-quality clustering. In *Proc. ICDE*, pages 685–694, 2002.

68. J. Pei, B. Jiang, X. Lin, and Y. Yuan. Probabilistic skylines on uncertain data. In *Proc. VLDB*, pages 15–26, 2007.

69. C. Ré and D. Suciu. The trichotomy of having queries on a probabilistic database. *The VLDB Journal*, 18(5):1091–1116, 2009.

70. M. A. Soliman and I. F. Ilyas. Ranking with uncertain scores. In *Proc. ICDE*, pages 317–328, 2009.

71. M. A. Soliman, I. F. Ilyas, and K. C.-C. Chang. Top-k query processing in uncertain databases. In *Proc. ICDE*, pages 896–905, 2007.

72. T. T. L. Tran, A. McGregor, Y. Diao, L. Peng, and A. Liu. Conditioning and aggregating uncertain data streams: Going beyond expectations. *Proceedings of the VLDB Endowment*, 3(1):1302–1313, 2010.

73. T. T. L. Tran, L. Peng, B. Li, Y. Diao, and A. Liu. Pods: A new model and processing algorithms for uncertain data streams. In *Proc. ACM SIGMOD*, pages 159–170, 2010.

74. D. Xin, H. Cheng, X. Yan, and J. Han. Extracting redundancy-aware top-k patterns. In *Proc. ACM SIGKDD*, pages 444–453, 2006.

75. D. Xin, J. Han, H. Cheng, and X. Li. Answering top-k queries with multi-dimensional selections: the ranking cube approach. In *Proc. VLDB*, pages 451–462, 2006.

76. J. Xu, Z. Zhang, A. K. H. Tung, and G. Yu. Efficient and effective similarity search over probabilistic data based on earth mover's distance. *Proceedings of the VLDB Endowment*, 3(1):758–769, 2010.

77. K. Yi, F. Li, G. Kollios, and D. Srivastava. Efficient processing of top-k queries in uncertain databases. In *Proc. ICDE*, pages 1406–1408, 2008.

78. Q. Zhang, F. Li, and K. Yi. Finding frequent items in probabilistic data. In *Proc. SIGMOD*, pages 819–832, 2008.

79. T. Zhang, R. Ramakrishnan, and M. Livnya. Birch: An efficient data clustering method for very large databases. In *Proc. ACM SIGMOD*, pages 103–114, 1996.

80. W. Zhang, X. Lin, Y. Zhang, W. Wang, and J. X. Yu. Probabilistic skyline operator over sliding windows. In *Proc. ICDE*, pages 1060–1071, 2009.

81. X. Zhang, K. Chen, L. Shou, G. Chen, Y. Gao, and K.-L. Tan. Efficient processing of probabilistic set-containment queries on uncertain set-valued data. *Information Sciences*, 196:97–117, 2012.

82. A. Zhou, C. Jin, G. Wang, and J. Li. A survey on the management of uncertain data (in chinese). *Chinese Journal of Computers*, 32(1):1–16, 2009.

Index